Berlin

Elbe River

Saale River

Leipzig

Naumburg

Jena

hau

Dresden

SAXONY

T0161322

Anni

Letters & Writings of
Annemarie Wächter

Edited by Marianne Wright and Erna Albertz

THE PLOUGH PUBLISHING HOUSE

Published by The Plough Publishing House
of Church Communities Foundation, Rifton, NY 12471, USA
and by Church Communities UK
Robertsbridge, East Sussex TN32 5DR, UK

ISBN: 978-0-87486-854-8

All photographs from Church Communities International Archives.

Library of Congress Cataloging-in-Publication Data

Arnold, Annemarie, 1909-1980.
    Anni : letters and writings of Annemarie Wächter Arnold / edited by
Erna Albertz and Marianne Wright.
       p. cm.
    Translated from unpublished letters originally written in German.
    Rev. ed. of: Youth movement to Bruderhof.
    ISBN 978-0-87486-854-8
  1. Arnold, Annemarie, 1909-1980--Correspondence. 2. Arnold,
Annemarie, 1909-1980--Diaries. 3. Bruderhof Communities. I. Albertz,
Erna, 1979- II. Wright, Marianne, 1977- III. Arnold, Annemarie, 1909-1980.
Youth movement to Bruderhof. IV. Title.
    BX8129.B68A6822 2010
    289.7092--dc22
    [B]

                                 2010030044

Printed in the U.S.A.

This book is dedicated to Annemarie's children:
Roswith
Johann Christoph
Maria
Edith
Lisa
Monika
Else

and in memory of Emmy Maria
and Marianne

Contents

Foreword

Dear Reader,

The writings in this book were only discovered after my mother's death. Astonishingly enough, until then neither my father nor I as only son knew of their existence. Reading them for the first time, it was remarkable to be able to meet my mother as a young woman through her correspondence with her family and various friends, and even more personally through her diary, and we marveled at the depth and openness of her thinking.

Inspired by what we had found, we shared her correspondence within our family circle and with friends. In the ensuing years we began to hear more and more often from young people–and especially from young women–how much my mother's life spoke into their own turbulent youth years. And so I am very thankful that this book will now make my mother's exchange of thoughts and ideas accessible to an even greater audience. We remain grateful to my mother's brother, Reinhold Wächter, who preserved these letters for over half a century and then sent them to us after she died.

During the time period between the two world wars which these letters span, Germany stood at a critical point in its history. Although the First World War had created an entire generation of wounded, distressed, and disillusioned young people, a vision and hope for a new and better world awoke in many and came to expression in the German Youth Movement, in which my mother participated. Tragically, this idealism and optimism was exploited by the Nazis only a short time later, as they enlisted these same youth to serve their terrible purposes. Only very few living in Germany at the time found another way, and for those who did it meant renunciation and suffering. For my mother, making the decision to follow this other way cost her many struggles.

Our world today is certainly just as exciting and full of challenges. In my role as author and youth pastor, I meet thousands of students of all ages each year. They all yearn just as strongly for meaning and fulfillment in their lives. They, too, wish for true friends and honest relationships and for more than that–they want to make a positive difference in this world and change it for the better.

You may be asking yourself what the thoughts and impressions of a young student from the turn of the last century could possibly have to do with the questions and problems of today's youth. As you begin reading, you will realize that it is my mother's honesty about her searching that makes this book a signpost for a disheartened generation. I hope that many will recognize themselves amongst its lines.

As a young woman, my mother longed to find meaning and a purpose for her life. The basis of faith, hope, and love my mother later carried with her and pointed me to in all situations was largely built in those early years of her life. She taught me much. May this book encourage you, as well, to never give up your search for a fulfilled and meaningful life.

Johann Christoph Arnold

Rifton, August 2010

Editors' Note

Anni was a prolific writer. Her weekly letters to her mother and sister, which frequently exceeded a thousand words, are a valuable record of 1920s Germany with their descriptions of daily life, accounts of educational trips around Germany, and commentary on events of the day. We have included a representative sampling of these letters, leaving some out entirely and shortening many others. Complete manuscripts of all the letters are available in the Church Communities International Archives.

In translating Anni's writing from the original German, we have attempted to preserve the youthfulness, individuality, and candor of her voice. We have also preserved the ambiguities in some of the letters and diary entries.

I.

Childhood

The baby was christened Anna Marie Lina Hedwig Wächter, but to her family she was just "Anni." Her arrival on Sunday, October 24, 1909 was a complete surprise to her older brothers and sister. They listened in amazement as their father and the midwife announced the happy news, and then all three – Reinhold (eight), Hilde (ten), and Otto (twelve) – tiptoed into their mother's room to see the baby sleeping in a lace-curtained bassinet.

Anni was now the youngest member of a large and happy household. In addition to their own children, Anni's parents had the care of over a hundred boys. These were students who came from all over Germany to attend the boys' boarding school of which Anni's father, Dr. Christian Otto Wächter, was the director. The students lived, studied, and played under one roof with the Wächter children. The house was seldom quiet.

Dr. Wächter had begun teaching in the Keilhau school in 1895, having come from a nearby town where his father, an amateur composer, had been mayor. The

*village of Keilhau, population ninety, is picturesque and
remote—it is accessible by only one road, which ends at
the end of the village—and Dr. Wächter was still considered something of a newcomer. Not so his wife. Hedwig
Wächter was the daughter and granddaughter of the
school's previous directors, and the great grandniece of its
founder, the philosopher, philanthropist, and educational
reformer Friedrich Fröbel.*

*Fröbel, best known for establishing the world's first
kindergarten, had opened the Keilhau school in 1817
as a place where he could put his educational ideas into
practice. "A child who plays thoroughly and with determination until he is too tired to continue will surely be
a thorough, determined man, capable of self-sacrifice for
the promotion of the welfare of himself and others," he
proclaimed. Accordingly, unstructured play in natural
surroundings formed an important part of the school's
curriculum. Anni's older brother Reinhold, describing
life as a student, later wrote, "It is strange, but school
work was not important for us. At least, it was no more
important than our life together, both among ourselves
as pupils and with the teachers. Those were the things
that mattered to us. That is part of the nature of a Fröbel
school. Its aim is formative and educational rather than
merely academic."*

*At the Keilhau school, academics were dealt with in
the morning. To start the school day, Dr. Wächter led a
brief worship service, which was followed by lessons in
conventional subjects. This done, all students formed a
line in front of a table where Frau Wächter was cutting*

bread. Each helped himself and then raced off for an hour of outdoor pursuits. The midday meal at one o'clock was preceded by an inspection, conducted by Dr. Wächter, of the cleanliness of each boy's hands, clothes, and hair. Afternoons were devoted to practical activities. In addition to sports and swimming, the boys were encouraged to spend long hours in the surrounding woods, where they built elaborate huts in which they could play. In Fröbel's philosophy, the educational value of these activities was immense:

To climb a new tree means the discovery of a new world to a boy. The outlook from above shows everything so different from the ordinary cramped and distorted side view. Not less significant is the boy's inclination to explore caves and ravines and to ramble in dark forests. It is the urge to find the new, to see and discover the hidden. From these rambles the boy returns with rich treasures of unknown stones and plants, of creatures – worms, beetles, spiders, and lizards – that dwell in darkness and concealment. "What is this? What is its name?" are questions to be answered, and every new word enriches his world and throws light upon his surroundings.

The Wächter children grew up happily in this setting, despite having to share their parents with dozens of boys. Dr. Wächter was a father figure for his students, many of whom called him "Papa" and addressed him with the familiar "Du," an unheard-of familiarity at that time. A reserved and quiet man, he loved music and delighted in arranging evening concerts for a family string quartet; Reinhold and Anni were somewhat reluctant performers at these events. Frau Wächter, responsible for the management of a busy household, had few free moments. In Reinhold's memory, "I hardly ever saw my mother walking slowly. She was always on the go, from five or six in the morning until ten or eleven at night. She had to wake all the maids early. A large staff was needed to prepare the meals and keep the house clean. It was a big house with rooms on many floors. The whole day long she was going up and down the stairs. My mother was exact and conscientious, very strict about order and cleanliness." The school was largely self-sufficient. Its vegetable garden employed many of the Keilhau villagers, and a forester-hunter was engaged to manage its several hundred acres of woodland.

Anni's parents were committed to Fröbel's ideals and his vision of childhood. To them, working in the Keilhau school was a calling, a noble inheritance, and they considered it a matter of course that their own children would in turn dedicate their lives to cultivating Fröbel's "garden for children." Each of the Wächter children held a share in the family partnership that owned and operated the school; this partnership had been passed down in the family for over a hundred years.

Then war broke out in Europe. In 1915, Germany was on the offensive, and seventeen-year-old Otto Wächter volunteered to fight. After a brief training, he was dispatched to Priesterwald, a densely forested region sloping up from the Mosel Valley that would come to be known as the "Forest of Death." By the time Otto arrived in mid-July, most of the trees had been flattened in the vicious fighting. German and French soldiers traded artillery fire, the French repeatedly charging the German trenches, only to be driven back. The combat was desperate, brutal, and ultimately futile: neither side advanced significantly during a year of fighting. In the midst of war, Otto did not forget his home. Postcards and gifts, addressed "Fräulein Anni Wächter, The Children's Room," arrived in Keilhau. "Dearest little Anni-sister," he wrote to her, "on the picture on the card you can see our gallant crown prince, who is trouncing the wicked French. Goodbye, my dear Annichen. Play happily with Erika and your other little friends. From your soldier-brother, Otto."

A little over a week after his arrival at the front, Otto was killed in battle. To five-year-old Anni, this was an incomprehensible event. Otto had been her particular champion, lovingly protective of the sister he called "Pummel" because of her short stature. Now he was snatched from her world by forces she could not understand. Anni grieved for her older brother, naming her favorite doll "Ottchen" in his memory. In other ways, though, the war remained a remote disturbance from her child's perspective. Battles and soldiers were far off, and even the starvation that afflicted most civilians as the war went on was kept at bay by produce from the school's garden and Frau Wächter's determination in providing for her household. Of more immediate concern to Anni in 1916 was starting first grade, an event which she later *described in an account of her childhood written for a school class:*

When I was six, I entered the village school. I felt very proud the first time I walked there with my slate, and I liked going to school very much. During the three years I attended the village school I became very connected to the village children. I wanted to be just like them in the way I dressed, the way I talked, and the expressions I used. For this reason I also spoke the local dialect by preference. In summer I was very sad that I wasn't allowed to go barefoot like the others, and I considered it a shocking disgrace that I had to wear shoes and stockings.

Anni left the village school when she was nine and began attending the Keilhau boarding school, where she was the only girl in her class.

At first there were only four in my grade and from the beginning we were like a band of comrades. So I gradually drifted away from the village children, probably in part because they left school earlier. Up until then, one of the village girls had still been my friend, but now I ended up playing only with boys. Until I was in seventh grade, I always wished I were a boy.

Because I had no other girls to play with in the years between fourth and seventh grades, I found great pleasure in reading. I devoured any book I could get hold of and read each of my own books at least twenty times. I did not especially care for sentimental girls' stories, preferring romantic tales of robber knights and, above all, stories about American Indians. Indian stories were the highest and best, and Karl May's *Winnetou* made a tremendous impression on me. I liked the stories about Indians so much because they depicted such outlandish things, foreign to my experience, and because no limits were set to such fantasies. I always had a lively imagination of what I would do if I lived among the Indians.

These stories absorbed and excited me to the extent that, especially in the evenings, I imagined an Indian, a robber, or a murderer waiting to fall upon me from behind every tree or in every dark corner. Of course these books influenced my play very much as well, and particularly during my vacations I lived, spoke, and wrote as if I were an Indian. One or two boys usually stayed at school during the vacation, and luckily they were the kind of boys who were just as full of fantasy as I and with whom I could dream up the most marvelous games.

My vacations were always divided between playing Indians and playing with dolls. Especially during the Christmas holidays I played doll family all day long. And the same boys who had played bloodthirsty Winnetou games with me during fall vacation now played peacefully at being the doll father. Even though I wanted to be quite warlike, I had a great love for my dolls and was very tender with them.

For the children at the Keilhau school, life – and the life of the imagination – remained shielded from a war that left over two million Germans dead. A period of polit-

ical agitation and uncertainty followed as the shattered country began to piece itself back together again. But by the time Anni's parents celebrated their twenty-fifth wedding anniversary on April 16, 1920, they could begin to think hopefully of the future. The school had flourished under their care: the number of students had increased, new buildings had been purchased and old ones restored, and a new school house had been built. Despite their grief at Otto's death and worry over Hilde's health – she was frail and often ill – the parents could rely on Reinhold and Anni, both promising scholars, to take on the family position as head of the highly regarded school, which had celebrated its hundredth anniversary three years before with a visit from the Princess of Schwarzburg-Rudolstadt.

But tragedy struck again in 1922. Dr. Wächter died unexpectedly at the age of fifty-eight after a sickness that lasted only a few days. His death, like Otto's, was incomprehensible to Anni, the more so since death, and the nameless fear and sorrow filling her twelve-year-old heart, were not considered suitable topics for discussion. Dr. Wächter's love for his children had expressed itself in little gestures of affection – a poem written for a birthday, shared laughter at some private joke, a bedtime serenade on his cello – and his death left a painful absence in their lives.

Now in addition to overseeing the household, Frau Wächter was forced to arrange for the directorship of the school. All the more, she pinned her hopes for the future on her daughter. Anni excelled at her studies despite feeling that, "it certainly wasn't pleasant that I was always expected to be the top of the class and be held up as an example to the others. Up to the seventh grade it didn't matter at all that I was a girl in a class of boys; it was all the same to everyone – we were just comrades. But in the following two years things gradually changed: I was simply not a boy. Gradually a separation arose, partly because several in my class were new, some of them from the city, and they introduced a new tone. I didn't care for this and kept away from them. Only the four of us from the old clan of the fourth grade remained good friends till the end."

At that time, Keilhau and her childhood circle made up Anni's whole world. She describes her uncomplicated view of life:

I had no opinion of my own – I just accepted everything and thought things had to be the way they were. I was not concerned with the problems of life; I simply existed and responded to whatever came my way. Added to this was the fact that at my home no one spoke about life's problems. People were very closed and reserved in that respect – they were hesitant to speak to each other about things that occupied them inwardly. I think this also explains my fear of All Soul's Day, especially after my father's death. On that day people were more inclined to come out of themselves; at other times they were very reserved and did not display emotion.

Since this was the only life I knew, I thought that things must be pretty much the same everywhere to how they were in Keilhau. I clearly remember that in ninth grade, around Easter, one of the boys said to me, "You'll be shocked when you get to the school in Naumburg–that's a whole different kettle of fish." "I don't believe it," I replied.

Because I didn't go on any trips, I had no contact at all with the outside world. Although many people visited us, they either didn't concern me or they appeared to fit very well into my little world of Keilhau. They didn't bring in anything new. Since I wasn't allowed to read any books other than books for young people until I was in ninth grade, I didn't find out anything from that side either.

Through her studies, however, a wider world began to open up.

My favorite subjects in school were drawing, singing, German, biology, chemistry, and math. In chemistry and biology I learned how things had come to be and about the underlying interdependence between everything. I thought this was very beautiful. In geography the same thing intrigued me as in the Indian stories, that is, I learned about things that until now I had never seen or experienced, things in which my imagination could be given free reign. I had great delight in daydreaming about such things.

My time in Keilhau came to an end with the exams at the end of ninth grade. I wanted to continue my studies, and so I left home to attend preparatory school.

2.

Leaving Home

In fall of 1925, Anni left Keilhau and enrolled in the Städtisches Luisen Oberlyceum, *a girls' academy in the city of Naumburg. Here she began the three-year course of studies that would make her eligible to take the* Abitur *exam, which she needed to pass before entering university. Anni's long-term plan was to earn a doctorate in education so that she would be able to take on responsibilities at Keilhau. To her family, these studies were an investment in the future of the Keilhau school. Payment of her tuition and living expenses was only possible through Frau Wächter's careful management of household finances.*

The academic requirements for Abitur candidates at the Oberlyceum were substantial, including classes for all three years in history, natural science, earth science, mathematics, religion, German, French, English, and Latin, as well as drawing, music, gymnastics, and handwriting. The school was progressive in its methods and emphasized the importance of critical thinking. More significant for fifteen-year-old Anni than her school work, though, was the experience of living away from home for the first time. The years of the Weimar Republic were a time of social and intellectual upheaval in Germany's cities and universities, and Anni was soon confronted by a world of ideas that she had not known existed. Because Naumburg was two hours from Keilhau by train, she returned home only for vacations. She later described the effects of this new arrangement:

A new world surrounded me in Naumburg. In the first place, I was now of course in a class of all girls. I had lately been wishing for that, since in the last months at Keilhau the boys had come to seem so coarse and crude. But I was sadly disappointed, because the girls were exactly like those city boys I hadn't liked. I tried to fit in with them and convince myself that all the things they thought were so marvelous really were marvelous. But I was disappointed and felt quite unhappy in that role. I also reacted against how in Keilhau I had always been forced to set a good example, and very much enjoyed getting into mischief and being very cheeky and absurd. Those were the years of adolescence. I wanted to "live" and, when I had worked myself up into all sorts of excesses, I thought it was real life.

Now I was listening to a lot of music and in the beginning I had an out-and-out hunger for it. It was all the same to me whether I listened to good or bad music; I only had a desire for masses of sound and noise. Above all I enjoyed listening to string music.

Because the world in which I now lived was so different

from Keilhau, I began to criticize everything and then rejected my old world. It seemed too simple to me. During this time I became somewhat estranged from my mother and sister.

Then suddenly this newly built up world was smashed. I began to feel that it was of primary importance that I become more self-controlled. I was looking for something new for my life. At that time the book *Drude* by Gertrud Prellwitz influenced me a great deal. Her words about friendship made an enormous impression on me. I wanted to strive for the light, for purity, and for truth.

Drude is the story of a teenage girl at a boarding school who is encouraged by her teachers to seek nobility and truth within herself and to pass on her insights to other students who are less enlightened. By this means, they assure her, she will participate in the approaching springtime of humanity, when–freed from bourgeois inhibitions–mankind will attain its true greatness. Anni paraphrased several passages from Drude *in her diary.*

D I A R Y

June 15, 1926

Friendship means a common search for the way of the good in which the one loves the other so much that he does not become cold if the other takes a false step. Always be full of light, always more light, always as full of light as you can. It is often so difficult to decide what is right and wrong, but still it is quite simple to find the way – you must always choose that which has more light. Exaggerated love leads to disorder. To go away from something that has become false doesn't help: you have to put it in order. Climb into the midst of it, then rise higher – that is the way. We must not be disappointed; we must act. All strength in us comes from God, and if it seems bad to us, the reason is that at that moment it is coming from a lower sphere and pulling us down and burdening us. Then we should struggle fervently until the strength is transformed and becomes light.

A person is not pure merely by being untouched. One must become untouchable. To be pure is a positive power that continuously renews itself. A person must always be completely truthful toward himself and others. One cannot be the type of person who treats his soul like a child that he stuffs with sweets but never washes. If a person keeps the goal in sight, he will of himself strike out in the right direction.

Art emerges when someone approaches a matter as if the salvation of the whole world depended on just this one thing being made good. Anything else is dilettantism, which must not be. Art that is not true is sin.

To Anni, the concept of life as a quest for truth was exhilarating and inspiring. As she later explained, "It was through the ideas in this book that I encountered the strivings of the Youth Movement."

The German Youth Movement was a post-war movement of young people seeking a way of life that could be lived truly and wholeheartedly. This search took widely varying forms–the Youth Movement included anarchists, back-to-nature enthusiasts, artisans, religious aesthetes, pagans, vegetarians, and poets. Property, social hierarchies, industrialization–these, the Youth Movement believed, were the root causes of injustice. Turning their backs on the cities, groups of young people banded together in villages, fields, and woods, seeking to experience truth in nature. Conventional social forms were replaced by folk traditions and culture, and formal manners gave way to frank exchanges of thought.

D I A R Y

July 25, 1926

Hah! They are dancing in the next room, and they want to make me dance with them, but I'm not going to let them force me. So that makes me an old maid, as if people's happiness depended on dancing. Real dancing would be one thing, but this stupid shoving around! If it were folk dancing–but this! Meantime I went for a walk with Hilde, and the woods were so beautiful–everywhere you see wonders incarnate, as if in a fairy tale. I love this land so much! Every flower is like a holy miracle, indescribably beautiful. I only keep wishing Lilo were here so that we could share all of this.

Lilo (Liselotte Lühr) was a classmate who shared Anni's enthusiasms, and together they started attending meetings of a Youth Movement group in Naumburg, learning the folk songs and dances that the Youth Movement had revived, and taking lengthy hikes through the Saale Valley's hills, forests, and meadows. Anni later described these experiences:

Many things were different in an outward way from conventional society. Dress and clothing were very simple. The girls wore full skirts with no decorations or lace, but mostly plain, bright colors like green, blue, red, or orange. The boys wore plain-colored shirts, a bit like a tunic. No one wore high heels, but ordinary flat shoes or sandals.

The young people could not stand the polite forms of the ordinary bourgeois world, so their way of speaking was plain and direct. In Germany, perhaps more than in other countries, you always had to say all the titles of a person—*Doktor* and *Ministerialrat* and *Professor,* three or four titles. You had to be sure to put them in the right order and not forget one of them. This kind of thing I found ridiculous and also boring. Young people revolted against this stiff, pretentious behavior.

My friend belonged to a small group of young people, boys and girls, who met once or twice a week. We used to sing together, and one of them would play guitar. We would also read together. Some circles in the Youth Movement were specifically Christian, but the circles I met with were not Christian. Yet they were all seeking something. They were not satisfied with life as it was—just having a job and making money. They often saw need in the city slums, like destitute children, and they asked the question: what can be done, what should be done, what is behind all this? Many longed to put their life to use, to serve somebody, children or the poor. We read the works of Weber and Ibsen and others who point to the need of the people and to the injustice in the world, and I felt a response in my heart.

They asked, "Is there a God?" I think most of them believed that there is a power in the universe that formed man's life, but people were in various stages of belief and disbelief.

The search for a unifying life force was an essential element of the Youth Movement. Distrustful of conventional Christianity, many looked for this life force in nature, exalting the might of wind, water, and mountains. They saw the sun, with its properties of light, heat, and purifying fire, as an especially potent symbol of the spiritual reality lying behind nature. Such feelings led some back to paganism and Germany's ancient folk religions. But for others, reverence for nature became a confirmation of genuine faith in Christ, sweeping away stale religious customs.

The Youth Movement's chief festival was the summer solstice, the day of the year when the sun's power is at its zenith. This was a day to spend beyond the reach of civilization, and groups of youth would wander to hilltop meadows to dance, talk, sing, and, as evening came, stand around gigantic bonfires. Anni and Lilo attended such an event at the end of their first year of preparatory school, just days before Anni was to return to Keilhau for the summer vacation.

17

June 23, 1926

Summer solstice celebration! At the Odin hut from five o'clock in the afternoon until two forty-five in the early morning. I have never experienced anything like it. It was one of the most beautiful days of my life.

We met at the appointed place (Lilo was along of course) and hiked to the Odin hut. There were about thirty people up there, all wonderful people. First we relaxed after the strenuous hike. Then we began folk dancing and danced almost without a break until ten o'clock. There was such joy present, completely natural and true. It was wonderful! The spirit of community was brought to expression through the dancing. Everyone had one and the same goal.

The funniest part was definitely the sack race and other races. We laughed until we cried. Holst fell headlong in his sack, which was naturally much too narrow for him, and could hardly get on his feet again. It was wildly funny. A puppet show had even been brought along and was performed brilliantly. The heads were carved out of rough pieces of wood and painted.

Then came the most beautiful part of the evening, the huge, huge fire. As it flared high, we joined hands in a chain and walked around the fire in the midst of the shower of sparks. Then Pasche said something that made you feel that we all had the same goal and were united in it:

Flame, free us from everything that is evil in us;
make us free from it, O Flame.
Let us not seek to rule and lord it over others.
Flame, let your glow fill our souls and consume us.
Flame, become ever greater in us.
Thou, Flame, make us free, pure, and good!

Lilo and I clasped each other's hands because that is what
we wish for – that the flame, the light, becomes stronger
in us.

Then we stood and let the fire, the holy fire, soak into
us. The glow made our faces burn, but I wanted to absorb
as much as possible of the great flame so that I would
be completely consumed by it. Everyone was silent and
looked into the fire, and what Pasche had said was like a
vow spoken for all of us. Later he read from *Faust* about
the eternal light. I had a feeling that was so strong, so free
and pure, that I believe that it was truly life.

Then we sat around the fire and sang, Lilo and I by the
dear Holsts. The fire gradually burned lower, and then
we jumped over the flames together. It was a wonderful
feeling to fly over the fire, and we did it many times. The
smoke stung our eyes, but that has to be part of it. The
puppets Kasperle and Jumbo the elephant were brought
out again, and then we sat around the fire and sang and
sang. Holst sang to guitar accompaniment with his beautiful mellow voice. I like both the Holsts so much. At
times a great sadness came over me, because this would
be the last time for six weeks. But then I thought: live

every moment and absorb all, all that is beautiful. This gave me such a blissful feeling that I thought my heart would burst. I clasped my hands together so that the bliss could find expression somehow.

Finally at 1:15 a.m. we got ready to hike back, after we had sung the beloved nightingale round. We took a wonderful path down to the Napoleon Stone. Torches lit our way, but in front of us the night was dark. It was as if we were walking on a quiet, soft path into infinity. No one knew where the path was leading us; we just walked and walked. It was so, so wonderful.

When we reached the highway, we again formed rows and sang lively hiking songs. That made me so happy. Now the moon went along beside us. The deeper we descended into the valley, the more mysteriously the mists from the Saale River swirled around us.

Again a great sense of bliss came over me. There was such a feeling of solidarity among us. What good, fine people were there. It was slowly growing light, and we parted at the same place we had met. I can't begin to say what this day meant to me. I will never, never forget it, because it was an experience! How unspeakably beautiful it is to live and to experience life!

I can understand very well how one can feel drawn to the Youth Movement, because that was its good spirit, which, I believe, has also gripped me now. Yes, it definitely has!

A year later Anni wrote:

The summer solstice celebration in June 1926 was decisive and made it clear to me where I belonged. I tried to strive for these ideals. I felt at peace now because nothing in me was exaggerated or inflated.

In the fall of 1926, Anni moved to different lodgings in Naumburg. Her new roommate was Irmgard Blau, who had just come from Halle to attend the Oberlyceum. Irmgard was a lively thinker, always questioning conventional values and ideas. She and Anni soon became inseparable; their classmates took to calling them "Blau & Wächter, Inc." Debates about art, truth, integrity, the existence of God–these were the substance of Anni's friendship with Irmgard. Decades later, Irmgard recalled:

The whole rest of my life, I never again experienced such a friendship, a friendship that simply grew between us. To have such a friendship is an extraordinary experience. I cannot remember that we ever had a serious quarrel.

In school we arranged that we were allowed to sit next to each other, and we did the school work in our own streamlined way: we made it simpler for ourselves. We did all our lessons as a team, taking turns so that only one of us did the written work, for example in translating or mathematics. This was tolerated in this very humanitarian school. We shared everything companionably and, while studying, refreshed ourselves with great quantities of apples and oranges bought cheaply. We also shopped for other things together–guitars with which to sing folk songs, and other objects we needed for our apartment.

My chief interest was the study of religion. I concerned myself with the theology of Friedrich Gogarten, a friend of Karl Barth. It fascinated us both. I had studied a book of his, *The Religious Decision.* Naturally, such a thing had to be discussed by the two of us into the early hours of the morning. We knew he lived nearby, so one Sunday we decided to visit him. He invited us to join him for coffee, and then asked us, "What do you want to become?" I answered "a professor" or some such elevated calling. "Ah," he said, "first learn to cook!" So our grand ideas were somewhat deflated.

Instead of the usual examination essay for the Abitur, we were given the option to work on a larger project of our own choice during the school year. I wrote about the history of the Youth Movement. Anni chose the theme, "My House." She described in great detail, with drawings, how she would build her future house. We supported each other in these projects and had a lot of fun.

In the winter months we studied for the Abitur together—not under a boring electric light but by romantic candle light. We used candle sticks from the woodworking shop of Herr Lamberty. We were frequent visitors to his shop, where we purchased defective candle-sticks, which were best suited to our finances.

Irmgard's Abitur thesis gives an insight into the girls' understanding of the Youth Movement and its signifi-cance for both of them. Irmgard begins by discussing the noble nature of manual work and the special role

played in society by the artisan. This theme was doubt-
less inspired by the above-mentioned Herr Lamberty, a
flamboyant Youth Movement figure whose group, the
Neue Schar, *had five years before been evicted from the*
Thuringian castle in which they were squatting amid
allegations of scandal. Now Lamberty had married and
settled in Naumburg to operate a turnery and craft shop
along Youth Movement principles. The central subject of
Irmgard's thesis, however, is the mystical and spiritual
aspect of the Youth Movement.

That which is beyond the rational is something eternal,
something of the other world. It awakens in people a
longing for the infinite and the struggle to become free
of what is earthly. This eternal quality is expressed in a
strong affirmation of life, for it gives people the strength
and desire for a purposeful fulfillment of their earthly
lives. In the Youth Movement this twofold striving–the
longing for a fulfilled life and liberation from the
finite–finds its strongest expression in its image of the
new man. Although things may look very different from
one branch to another or from one individual to another,
this is the common goal of the Youth Movement and is
reflected everywhere in it. And if we are concerned with
the Youth Movement's attitude to various areas of life,
we need to return to the longing for a new humanity. But
most of all it has to show in the attempt to create a new,
personal mode of life.

Powers that are beyond reason are most closely
connected to religion. The Youth Movement has an urge

to attain the eternal, not to remain stuck in the temporal. It has a respect for the depths of life that it cannot grasp. This is what we all have in common: we take religion seriously, we grapple with it, and more than that, it truly fills our lives. But since the Youth Movement affirms life so strongly, it carries its religion into its joy in earthly life.

Only a few will come to a crass rejection of all religion, because for most young people it is not the intellect that is essential, especially not when it comes to the question of the deepest meaning of life. Our religion is borne of mysticism. We come to faith only by direct experience.

What is the attitude of the Youth Movement to Christianity? We need to consider Christianity because this is the religious form that is most closely connected to our lives. If we in the Youth Movement are truly religious, we must differentiate our religion from the Christian faith of the church in a way that is truly our own. The difference is that all of us, regardless of what we think of God and the beyond, see the goal of a new humanity in this world. Thus our mysticism is not from above but from within. It does not distance itself from the struggle but is the driving, supra-rational force that stands behind our life purpose. If this were not the case, our new formation of human life would be merely a material, superficial improvement of the world.

There are others who cannot affirm Christianity because they have replaced Christian ethics with another code. I'm thinking primarily of the nationalistic direction which has the Germanic race and racial purity as its ideal. The emphasis on race is opposed to Christianity first of all because the Christian religion stems from Judaism and Jesus himself was a Jew. A deeper reason, however, is that the nationalistic view of different moral levels is incompatible with the Christian ethic which holds all people of equal worth.

Bit by bit, everything that pertains to our daily life has been renewed and permeated by our ideas. This took place unconsciously and as a matter of course. Thus our clothing is not a new fashion, created arbitrarily as many suppose; it developed from our whole lifestyle. It was soon noticed that it was absurd to hike with long hair and formal collars, and to the girls it was obvious that they couldn't dance and move freely in tight dresses. So the style of our clothing grew out of our feeling for naturalness and our desire for freedom. Precisely in the question of clothing the urge for community appears. That is why at our conferences and celebrations we like to wear bright, plain-colored clothing. The pure colors harmonize with each other, and through that means a bond is formed between people. However, a sense of community created by clothing would certainly be meaningless and ridiculous if it were not for this underlying truth: dress is a symbol of a person. Man should not confront the world as if he were an alien creature pitted against it. Rather, he must become one with it and must once again grasp the things around him as symbols. That is exactly what differentiates our clothing from fashion.

Art is decisive for the shaping of our life, because art means giving form to the living strength in or around us. To be an artist means the ability to bring what is within a person into contact with the outside world. This ability gives redemption from the inner, disorderly, chaotic powers, and the freedom to become more fully human. When we understand art in this way it follows that every person in the Youth Movement wants to be and should be an artist in some small way. We want to find these powers within us and bring them out, because only then will they have value. However, we don't want to seek these powers within ourselves alone (even if that is our first and foremost goal), but also to discover them in people of earlier times and in their works.

For this reason we have gone into the cities and stood before the Gothic cathedrals and sensed something of the spirit of the Middle Ages, the spirit of community. What attracted us in these symbols is the community of people who helped in the construction and together adored their God. In addition, we feel an affinity to their striving toward the eternal, their search for the transcendent. In the Gothic altarpieces we see the essence of art–not something to be copied but something that symbolically brings inner powers to expression. The characters on the gilded background contain something unearthly and holy; they are lifted above the world. So the Youth Movement must feel drawn to them, because it rose from the longing to flee the utilitarian, earthly life and discover again the powers in man that are beyond the rational.

But the Youth Movement cannot remain stuck in admiring works of art; it wants to create things itself and develop its own powers. For this reason it starts with the

earliest, most primitive art form, the folksong. Song is
the immediate expression of human experience–it lifts
us out of everyday life. It is an art form that, to a certain
extent, is possible for everyone. It is simple and natural.
But more important is the power of song to bind people
together in an expression of their common longing and
their common experience. Music joins people more
closely than any other art form or anything else can. In
singing together, people sway in rhythm and barriers
between them fall.

It is similar with the folk dance. In dancing, the rhythm
is the most powerful force. Dance is worship; it is liberation and surrender to life. The circle is symbolic for the
earliest folk dances, the closed ring of people of a single
purpose. Village children and young peasants are often
drawn into the circle, because anyone who wants should
take part in this community.

Our celebrations, however, do not take place for
outsiders–we celebrate them for ourselves because
through them our community grows closer. One such
feast that we celebrate for the sake of community is the
summer solstice. The purifying, liberating power of the
fire is a symbol to us of the will, of the inner powers
through which we overcome the finite in order to attain
deeper life. Fire frees people from the present and binds
them in a higher spiritual community. In the circle around
the fire we are no longer individuals. We become one
whole, a unity. We want to become part of the flame itself
and not simply observe it; therefore we jump through it.

For Anni, these ideas were transformational; an account she wrote of a summer trip to northern Germany shows the extent to which she had adopted a Youth Movement outlook.

Our Study Trip from June 18 – 26, 1927

Counting Fräulein Sauerbrey there were sixteen of us when we set out at noon on Saturday. We were very eager, for a completely new world was to be opened up to us. The closer we came to northern Germany, the more birch and pine trees there were, also broom, and whole woods of oak trees. In Lüneberg, Pasche was waiting for us at the station, and we walked through the town to our youth hostel at the marketplace. Meanwhile it had grown dark, and we had a fine view of the St. John's Church tower, which stood silhouetted against the sky. It was not built symmetrically but slightly crooked, which gave it a melancholy aspect.

Next morning we ran out to the heath in the rain. That was wonderful. The dark brown, heavy, soft heath with the storm-bent pine and the hanging birches. I have a feeling that the heath could be my home. The pines and birches are the secret of the heath and of the North German people altogether; on the one hand hard, somewhat brusque and firm, and on the other hand melancholy, sometimes mischievous, and gentle. The rain seemed to suit the landscape. The heath is for men to brood and dream over.

The St. John's Church gives the impression of a festival hall. You can't possibly get warm in there. It has an old organ that was played by Bach and Brahms and has recently been restored. We heard it being played, the *Propheten Fantasy* by Liszt, a fugue by Bach, and a piece by a recent Italian composer. This music brought something like a communal experience to our class, the only time on this trip. We then traveled on to Lübeck.

On seeing Lübeck's seven pointed spires coming into view, you feel right away that you are going to be good friends with this city. On the first morning we visited the St. Mary Church. As you enter, the contradiction between the church's original form and its ornamentation is an immediate irritation. The brick is whitewashed, and the whole church is overloaded with baroque figures and altars. Still, if you look closely, you can find quite a bit of fine artwork. First there is the *Dance of Death*, in which death is seen in twenty-four different forms of expression and movement. Then there is the *Burial of Christ* by Overbeck, a Lübeck painter, in very pure, brilliant, unearthly colors. The Christ seems to me too effeminate. On the whole, though, Overbeck's figures have great clarity, purity, and gentleness. They know what life is about. This receives especially beautiful expression in his Mary. There is inner peace and harmony and a dedicated, childlike faith on his figures' faces; they are strangers to despair.

The stained-glass windows in St. Mary's have been preserved in their original colors. There too is the *Darsow Madonna*, a late Gothic stone figure. Her features are

29

infinitely gentle, pure, moving, chaste. I have noticed when drawing how hard it is to express the gentleness of line. In the Lübeck Cathedral there is a counterpart to this Mary, but this one here is by far the more beautiful. In the sacristy there is an early Gothic carved wooden altar. The faces on these figures are not at all realistic, but they are so fine–naïve or childlike, devoted–just out of the master's singleness of heart. They are very uncomplicated.

Elsewhere in St. Mary's there are many wooden carvings, in part quite roguish and sometimes a bit crude. The Lübeck Cathedral is from early Gothic times. It has heavy, ponderous arches and also has whitewashed bricks. The fine thing about it is that the side naves in particular have no ornamentation, so they get their effect simply by the vaults and the weight of their form. It gave me the feeling of firm quietness, but that behind it all there is something that stands much higher and carries the whole. Here, too, there were late Gothic carved wooden figures, very expressive, and then a horrible Baroque altar.

After dinner Irmgard and I went to the St. Peter's Church lookout tower. We had a fine view over this entire Hanseatic city. It still gives a complete impression of a Hanseatic city with its many pointed red roofs and high towers. There is something so dignified about it, intimate, yet serious and businesslike, without anything hasty or nervous, but striving consciously toward a goal.

We then slept one more night in Lübeck and went on to Hamburg the next morning. There we took a tour all around the harbor. This was interesting at first, since quite a number of big ships were lying at anchor. But

basically the ships all look very much alike, and the individual harbors are not different from one another either.
I would not take a harbor tour like that so very often.

We then went on a steamboat on the Elbe to Blankenese.
The Elbe kept getting broader and broader at the end, so
that the shore was barely visible. The big sailboats looked
fine with their brown sails standing black against the sky.
Lilo and I went down to the beach and lay on the sand.
In front of us the water was quite silvery, and toward the
other side it was completely dark.

With Lilo I believe it is like this: we go along side by
side, but between us there is a deep pit, and only at times
there is a bridge across the pit where we find a resting
point. Then each one continues on her own way. That
evening was a resting point like that. I do not know how
this will go on. I can't help it, but sometimes I just can't
figure her out.

That was our last night in Hamburg. I felt very uncom-
fortable there. I had the feeling, what are you actually
doing here? You don't belong here. It seemed to me as
if the business at the Stock Exchange was what consti-
tuted the nature of Hamburg. I was very glad when we
left next morning. I could not live there. I wouldn't even
like to be there for a month.

The sea had a freeing effect after this constricted
feeling. The ocean altogether is something so magnificent and powerful that it makes you forget everything
petty and technical. There is such power in this element
that you wonder that it does not simply crush such a
wretched little human ship to pieces and throw it out. I

did not have the impression that the ocean consisted of water, but that it was a being with countless forms that enjoys changing itself every moment and showing its power in doing so.

We spent the evening philosophizing together in the reading room at the hostel, then left at three o'clock the next day and drove home, arriving at 8:00 in the morning.

As she was about to graduate from the Naumburg academy, Anni wrote:

Through my literature classes I learned about many things of which I had been previously ignorant. I have always been very dependent on the world around me. I made efforts to become freer. But I was often thrown back and forth, and through this I went from one extreme to the other. Now my longing is for inner freedom and truth.

The village of Keilhau around 1910. The main building of the boarding school is at the back of the picture on the right.

Childhood in Keilhau

The Wächter children, 1911. Hilde (12), Anni (2), Otto (14), Reinhold (10).

Anni and her older
sister Hilde.

Anni, age five.

Otto, age seventeen,
a soldier.

Inspection of Keilhau students' hands before a meal.

Ten-year-old Anni with her Keilhau boarding school class in 1919.

The Wächter clan and school staff at the silver wedding anniversary celebration of Anni's parents, April 16, 1920.

Dr. Christian Otto and Hedwig Wächter, Anni's parents.

Anni, 1925

Naumburg

Irmgard Blau, 1928

Summer Solstice celebration, June 23, 1926. Anni in center couple.

Sample pages from Anni's ninety-page Abitur thesis "My House" showing her drawing for the ground floor of a three-story house she planned, designed, and decorated.

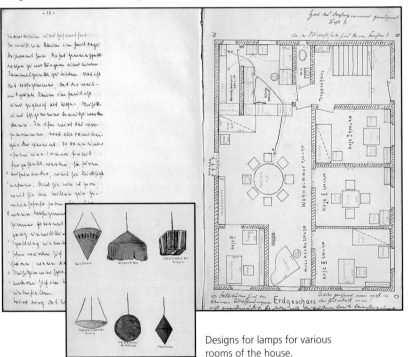

Designs for lamps for various rooms of the house.

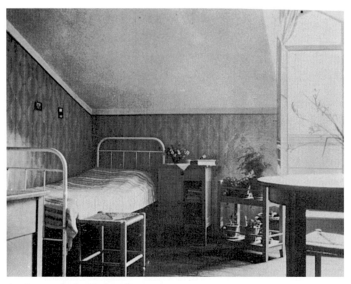
Anni's room in the Thale college.

Thale

[handwritten letter]

"Affectionate greetings for Sunday from your Anni."

Fräulein Dr. Kühn   Frau Direktorin Maria Keller   Emi-Margret Arnold

The Thale students and Hort children celebrating Frau Direktorin's birthday.

Eberhard and Emmy Arnold

View of the Sparhof from the Küppel.

The Sparhof

Else von Hollander
shortly before her death
in January, 1932.

Childcare at the Sparhof. Emi-Margret with daughter Heidi, left.

Anni with her mother and Reinhold during her July 1932 visit to Keilhau.

Annemarie's wedding to Heinrich Arnold, at the Liechstenstein community in March 1936.

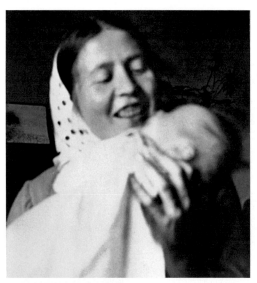

Later Life

Annemarie with her daughter Emmy Maria, at the community in England, 1938.

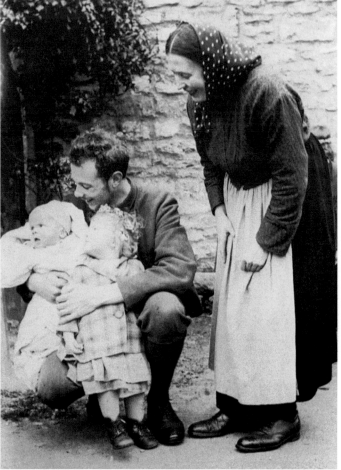

Heinrich and Annemarie with Roswith and Johann Christoph, at the community in England, 1941.

Annemarie with a children's group at the community in England.

The Arnold family at the community in Paraguay.
Roswith, Edith, Maria, Monika, Johann Christoph, Else, Heinrich, Annemarie, Lisa.

Annemarie reading to her youngest daughters Monika and Else at the Woodcrest community in upstate New York.

Annemarie in Woodcrest.

The Arnold family in Woodcrest. Heinrich, Annemarie, Roswith, Else, Johann Christoph, Oma Emmy Arnold, Edith, Lisa, Monika, Maria with her husband David Maendel.

Heinrich and Annemarie with their grandchild Nathan Maendel, Woodcrest, 1966.

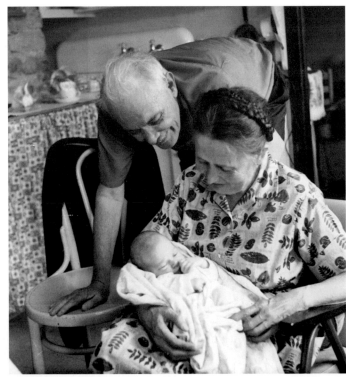

3.

Thale College

Anni had entered the preparatory school with the intention of continuing her studies at university. By the end of her third year, however, she had abandoned this plan and decided instead to pursue an earlier wish for a career caring for young children. As she later explained:

When I was thirteen I knew for the first time what I wanted to become. That summer my married cousin came for a visit with her baby and stayed the whole summer. The little girl was less than a year old and still very uncoordinated, but it was my greatest delight to take care of her. As soon as I had even a moment of free time, I spent it with her and cared for her, played with her, and took her for walks or did anything else I could for her. I neglected everything else for this: school work, practicing violin, playmates, visitors of my own age who came to us – all so I could be with this little girl. And that summer it became quite clear to me that I had to become a kindergarten teacher or something that had to do with children. The following year too, when the little girl was older, and later, when a little brother came along, my wish remained the same. I drifted a little from this idea in the ninth and tenth grades, but by the time I finished preparatory school I knew clearly that I wanted to become a Youth Director in a school or kindergarten.

To prepare herself for this, Anni enrolled in the Soziale Frauenschule, *a women's college in Thale. Founded in the years following World War I by Maria Keller, who remained the school's guiding spirit and its beloved* Frau Direktorin, *the college offered trainings that would enable young women to provide for themselves and contribute to society. A generation of men had died in the war, and many women would never be able to marry. In order to equip her students with the confidence they would need as single women, Frau Direktorin set a high tone at the college, selecting her staff only from upper class families. Students were required to curtsy whenever they saw a teacher, even if only at a distance.*

By the time Anni began classes in 1929, the school had around a hundred students and offered courses of study in social work, kindergarten teaching, home economics, and the administrative skills needed to manage a children's home or school (the so-called Jugendleiterinnen, *or "Youth Directors"). Although hands-on skills were emphasized (Anni received lessons in cleaning a bath tub and packing a suitcase), Frau Direktorin's main goal was to help each girl become a* Vollmensch—*a complete individual with the practical and inner resources for a fulfilled life. She took great personal interest in the spiritual and intellectual development of her students. To start the day she would read a passage from Fichte or another thinker to the whole student body; in the evenings the students took it in turn to select an enlightening quote to share and discuss. In an effort to awaken her students' social conscience, she regularly organized lectures by social workers from deprived areas. At other times the assembled student body would be given instruction in history, philosophy, and appreciation for the fine arts. "What artist might have drawn this picture?" "Which philosopher would have said that?" she would quiz the future kindergarten teachers and orphanage directors.*

Anni, who preferred being with children to administrating them, enrolled in a course of studies called Kindergarten-Hort, which qualified teachers to work with children ages two to fourteen. Hort, which literally means "a safe retreat" or "hidden place," refers to after-school programs for children of working mothers which were intended to provide an alternative to playing on the streets. Hort institutions, both private and public, had been common in Germany for several decades. The teachers in these institutions provided help with homework, supervised outdoor activities, and organized arts and crafts projects. Since the Thale college operated a kindergarten and Hort center, as well as a daycare facility for children of women who worked in a nearby ironworks factory, practical experience was plentifully provided. Anni enjoyed learning how to occupy, teach, and feed a group of small children, but her favorite class was child psychology and educational theory. The young professor, Fräulein Dr. Kühn, urged her students to think about essential questions of human nature and the place of the individual in the world, themes that had also occupied Anni's Youth Movement friends. Anni confided her thoughts on these questions to her diary:

D I A R Y

Thale, March 3, 1929

When does life really begin? This, of course, is not a worn-out question, it has to be asked again and again. Why can't one grasp it? And where is it, who lives it? Not us here. I believe that all that is left for us is self-forgetfulness, sleep. We have been waiting for it all the time. We try to deaden ourselves again and again through our intellect and consciousness. And it does not help. Earlier, I always imagined life meant joining hands and working together. But I can't do that. Because the consciousness that is instilled in us by school has killed everything with its intellectualism. It has done more harm than anyone can imagine. I only want to be able to be radical once, radical to the point of unconsciousness. People are never given time for this, they always have to be "mature" already. I only want for once not to be "I," to be quite far from myself and everything physical, to be able to rest. I want no fellowship, I want nothing, I want no obligations and no demands. I only want to rest and soar, or be a flower on a bright summer day.

And what then is God? I don't know whether I believe in him or don't believe in him. I cannot pray. I have only read about him. I would rather be an atheist than be like this. Once there has to be something that tears something in my heart, that takes a firm hold of me. I wish something would come that would tear me completely, so that I had physical pain and torment, so that it would make me forget everything about myself, so nothing would be left but the pain. But there are always onlookers there, who watch one with psychological sympathy.

Although Anni was uncertain about what she believed or even if she believed, she remained fascinated by religion. During her first year at the Thale college she studied the German mystics, writing detailed summaries of the works of Meister Eckhart, Tauler, and Suso. In a study of Martin Luther she posed the question, "What does mankind truly want from religion?"

Anni's search also led her to other writings. A reading journal which she kept for the year 1929 lists over sixty titles by authors including Dostoevsky, Oscar Wilde, Herman Hesse, Leo Tolstoy, Martin Buber, Jack London, Thomas Mann, and Upton Sinclair, as well as dozens of books of social and educational commentary. Important passages and ideas were copied into the journal, along with brief observations. Not all the books furthered the quest for truth. "Latrine atmosphere!" she wrote disgustedly next to one title.

In spring of 1929, the students in the Kindergarten-Hort class were required to write an extended essay on the theme, "Do children and fairy tales belong together?" Anni worked on this assignment for several months; the essay she turned in is more than four times as long as the summary printed here.

Children and fairy tales are inseparable—one cannot be imagined without the other. Children and fairy tales belong together in the deepest sense because the basic element of a fairy tale is living deeds. There is nothing abstract or intellectual in them; the focus is completely on the action of the story, and there is nothing senseless or unrelated in the plot.

Unburdened by rational thought and classifying, criticizing consciousness, primitive peoples could create and develop such themes. Therefore there is a naturalness, unconcern, and freshness to fairy tale characters that seems impossible to the modern, self-conscious person.

It is no longer possible for modern man to create stories in this way; the talent of an artist is necessary nowadays. But that does not mean modern man can no longer relate to fairy tales. These stories touch on something that is hidden deep within him, beneath all the strata of rational thought and mechanical knowledge.

The search for an absolute is never finished; it stirs people's hearts again and again and troubles the people of today just as much as it did the primitive people of long ago. A fairy tale, therefore, is not subject to the course of time: it springs from the eternal question of the spiritual existence of mankind, which modern man must also face above and beyond all the fantastic, strange, comical, and tragic elements of life.

Now we come to the question: Is there a particular spiritual connection between children and fairy tales? This question can be answered with a simple "yes," and this "yes" must be spiritually, inwardly founded in some way, since it would be completely contrary to the nature of a child to take a merely superficial liking to something. It only remains for us to discover how and why the strong relationship between children and fairy tales exists.

The whole being of a child is life-affirming, since the child itself is life, deeds. The child is in a constant process of making himself one with all things. He takes everything into himself: the natural world, humankind, the supernatural. This inward connection with all things means that a child can only believe in the fundamental good of it all. "The world is good," or "Everything categorically has to be led to a good end, to a good resolution." And that is, of course, exactly what we find again and again in every fairy tale. That's why it says, "and they lived happily ever after."

For the child and for the fairy tale there is always a resolution, a result. The child can't do otherwise than believe again and again in the power that arises from becoming one with all things. It is curious that the perceptions of an adult follow an exactly converse path. The adult seeks and struggles for fulfillment in life, but when it comes down to it knows that he is better off not reaching the goal because then it would all be over. The struggle and suspense, for the sake of which he believes his life to be livable at all, would then cease. Child and fairy tale both want–and find–fulfillment. They live in happiness that knows no end or disappointment, but they truly live.

In a fairy tale something is always happening. Every moment a new element, happening, or character appears. One need not speak of individual fairy tales here: they all share this attribute. This constant flow of movement, the unstoppable progression of the plot, again reflects the relationship to the child, whose life is activity and movement. It is really so: children and fairy tales are inseparable. To speak of one is to mean the other at the same time. Fairy tales can often be brutal and cruel–people and animals die–and yet, despite everything, the positive powers always win. There can be no other ending. Child and primitive man must always find such a resolution.

The only character in a fairy tale to suffer relentless punishment is the one that is the embodiment of evil. But that does not in and of itself mean anything distressing or oppressive–the deed is served its just reward. A sense of justice is extremely clearly developed. The fairy tale knows no compromise; it remains consistent. A child also possesses a very keen and unbending feeling for justice. The more uncomplicated and unstructured the fairy tale is, the more strongly are the two extremes displayed.

Anni's essay acknowledges the absolutes of good and evil found in fairy tales and the world of childhood. But the

*idea that enlightenment and excellence should come from
within still pursued her.*

March 8, 1929

Frau Direktorin told me that I am phlegmatic and
falling asleep, that I need more intensity and eagerness.
That something is demanded of us when we are here,
especially those of us who have passed their Abitur. I am
not sure how she means that, but I don't know where
I am supposed to get intensity and eagerness from. For
that, you need something to draw on. Still, she has been
quite open about everything, and now at least I can't
deceive myself anymore. For worst of all is the fact that
she possibly still has some hope that there may be something alive in me. (At least that is what she says, but I
almost think she says that only out of sympathy, and that
is much worse.)

But now I do know that it is a complete illusion that
I in myself am anything. Already in Naumburg I knew
that all the time, but I kept suppressing it, and Irmgard
also knew this about me, and also suppressed it. I thought
that after I left Naumburg this feeling would never come
back, but now it is like that again. If only I did not know
it! It would be better to live like an animal than always to
see and know that there is something deeper and yet to
realize that you can't attain it, that you are only deceiving
yourself all the time. I am supposed to master everything

in a living way, including my studies, but I am simply unable to. There is simply nothing in me, I am nothing, I have no opinion, no conviction, no direction, no nothing. Either everything I say is what I have learned, or I say what the others say and then go on thinking I found it within myself.

Weekly letters to her mother and sister, written at the same time as the diary, give no hint of this unhappiness. Lengthy and cheerful, they describe a lively and varied student life interspersed with short stays at the college's country retreat in nearby Treseburg and class trips to educational and welfare institutions throughout Germany. Anni devoted many hours to her correspondence with her family – the excerpts printed in this chapter are only half of what she wrote during the months of May and June, 1929.

Thale, May 4, 1929

Dear Mama and Hilde,

Thank you very much for your dear Sunday letter. For me this week has gone at a run. On Thursday we have to hand in our composition on fairy tales, and I will have to work industriously on that, but right now there's a little pause.

Yesterday evening our class met with Frau Direktorin and we discussed our summer plans. It is all figured out to the last day. It's certainly very nice to have a proper vacation in summer, although it's sad that it doesn't coincide exactly with ours at home. When we start in the after-school care department in September, we'll still learn all about summer activities and that will of course be very nice. During the time before our study trip we still want to go to Trautenstein near Hasselfelde once again. There is a children's home there and we want to spend a day observing how it is run.

By the way could you please send my bike right away or as soon as possible by freight. Please send the pump, bell, and if possible the carrying rack along in a parcel, but otherwise you can send it unpacked – that won't hurt it. But please oil it again beforehand. I could make very good use of it on trips, like to Trautenstein, Stiege, and so on. Frau Direktorin advised this to us very strongly. Yesterday we could also tell our wishes regarding practical work. I think that I will go to Gettenbach near Frankfurt am Main. Unfortunately it is quite a long trip and we have to pay it ourselves and won't get reduced tickets. But it is supposed to be very beautiful down there and I will definitely take a look at Frankfurt. Isn't that a good summer plan? We were delighted with it in any case.

Our May Day singing last Wednesday was very successful, we were very happy about it. Already early in the morning we were awakened by singing. We celebrated two birthdays this week. One was on the proper date, the other a late celebration, but both were very nice. When I look out of our window I look right down on a pair of light green birches – they look very festive. At the moment we are always looking out for flowers, wood anemones, figwort, and sometimes a few primulas already. I'm never sure where you can find them here because there aren't any meadows in this area. We've also worked a couple times in the garden, planting and setting things to rights. Now it looks very orderly.

Now a very affectionate Sunday kiss from your

Anni

What is Reinhold doing? The belt will be woven this week.

Thale, May 10, 1929

My dear Mama and Hilde,

Isn't it wonderful how suddenly spring has come, almost overnight? On Tuesday all the fruit trees suddenly began to bloom; I hadn't even noticed it and suddenly they all looked white. Now it's fun to look out of the window. The Bode Valley with the Witches' Dancing Ground and the Horse's Hoofprint doesn't look dead and gray anymore. On one of the days it turned as warm as summer and we ate dinner outside under the linden trees in front of the house. Everything had been carried out beforehand, and afterwards each of us took our plate and chair in with us so that it was all cleaned up faster than usual. Apparently we will eat out there often in summer.

Last Sunday we went out in the afternoon, lay down in the woods near a glorious view, and read and slept.

Lots of flowers are being picked these days–there are bouquets everywhere. The people coming from the retreat home at Treseburg always bring with them big bouquets of the pale yellow primroses that grow there along the Bode River. One hardly finds any here; you have to go looking quite far. It's also terribly fun to look for flowers with the kindergarten children. Now we've planted pansies and daisies with them in little beds, and sown carrots and Japanese lanterns. Each group has their little bed which they water with great delight.

I am currently still a substitute teacher in the kindergarten and don't have my own class. I have to take care of all the external details–bringing the groups their materials, washing the plates after meals, and helping out when something is happening in one of the groups. At the beginning I'm always pretty busy but later on I have more time to observe the different groups, and that of course is also very interesting and I learn a lot that way. Sometimes there are also children who are supposed to play by themselves and who I then have to look after. I enjoy it every time that happens.

From next week on I will have my own group again, hopefully a lively one. That is to say, we will not go to Treseburg next week but instead are supposed to stay in the kindergarten till Whitsun. And also then things will somehow still be organized differently. A few are supposed to get all the toys, etc. ready for the new Hort students, and only one or two of us will have the children. But it's all still very unclear. Frau Direktorin often comes down now to listen in, which is mostly very nerve-wracking. We hardly have any theory at all anymore, only one lesson per afternoon at the most.

On Thursday for Ascension Day most of the girls went to Treseburg and already spent a night there. They have also hiked further from there. Our class stayed here. There was a wonderful quiet in the house. Four of us (including me) had Sunday duties completely without teachers. We had to cook and prepare everything. It was enormous fun and the meal was delicious – we thought so at least.

In the morning of Ascension Day there was a real proper thunderstorm and then it poured like anything, a beautiful spring rain. It was so relaxing lying in bed and watching it. I don't know yet what will happen at Whitsun. Hopefully it will also be nice and quiet for you. I am happy that the grounds are so nicely back to rights again.

Now a very, very affectionate greeting for Sunday and a little kiss from your

Anni

Hopefully Sunday will be really beautiful for the two of you, with warm spring sunshine. I will have time all Sunday long to think of you.

With Irmgard Blau attending college in Halle, she and Anni saw each other only every few months. Fortunately, Anni discovered that many of her interests – from

educating children to reading Dostoevsky—were shared by one of her classmates in the Kindergarten-Hort class, Emi-Margret Arnold. The two became close friends, sharing a room in the second year at college. They enjoyed taking lengthy walks together, often going for hours without feeling the need to speak. When they did talk, Anni soon realized that Emi-Margret could identify with her desire for a life that was lived truly and freely. But for Emi-Margret, these were not just vague ideas, and in their many long discussions she told Anni about her family and the community she belonged to. This was a group of families and singles who were trying to live like the earliest Christians. In 1920 Emi-Margret's parents and aunt Else had started this venture by moving from Berlin to a farmstead in rural Germany. Already there were over fifty members at the community, which was known as the Sparhof. The basis for this radical lifestyle, said Emi-Margret, was belief in Jesus. While the life in community sounded like a Youth Movement dream come true, Anni found the religious basis less attractive. As she later recounted,

Emi-Margret told me some of the inner background of the community she came from, but I could not understand it. I sensed that Emi-Margret had a real belief in God, a firm basis, and that is what we discussed mostly, but I was afraid of it. I wanted to be very sure that this really was the truth and not that I would find out after a year or two that it was giving the appearance of being real when it actually was not. So I was somewhat critical, even though in another way I was attracted. I did not want to bind myself to any firm belief or to commit myself.

From her side, Emi-Margret wrote to her parents on May 1, 1929:

I talked for a long time with Anni about faithfulness, which for her is only a concept. For people who know nothing except the soul and its emotions, there is no such thing as faithfulness. It would take too long to write about it all. We have long and heated debates. But actually such a debate can only be described verbally. In a certain way she reproached me because I have a fixed center point in life from which I take my bearings. But at least she knows that I never, never want to lose this fixed point; I told her so.

For Emi-Margret, this "fixed point" was self-evident; the community she grew up in was founded to be an expression of faith. From her father, she had learned to admire the Youth Movement's vitality and joyful non-conformity while clearly seeing its shortcomings. In fact, Eberhard Arnold had written an article discussing the novels by Gertrud Prellwitz that had so impressed Anni, in which he concluded: "Emotion without Christ's spirit leads to the abyss."

Anni's correspondence with her family continued to describe only the activities of college life.

Thale, May 18, 1929

My dear Mama and Hilde, dear Reinhold,

I am sending you many warm greetings and wishes for Whitsun. Hopefully it will be a beautiful day for you. It just has to get a little warmer again – today it's really cool. Did many of the boys leave? Here quite a few who don't have to travel far have gone home for the Whitsun weekend. There won't be any activities here. From our class four have stayed, including Emi-Margret. But quite a few former students and teachers are coming to visit. I'm quite excited to see how it will all be.

On Saturday we had a splendid experience. Our house had a fire drill. A fire was simulated in the attic. Ladders were set up, the streets were barricaded, and the whole house was doused. Two of the girls were carried downstairs and saved. They were laid on the grass, and someone pretended to give one artificial resuscitation while the other had her arms and legs bandaged. There was a great commotion when the two appeared upstairs again. It was a terrifically funny business, with the whole house standing and watching from the windows.

By the way, my bicycle arrived here hale and hearty on Monday and I already put it to use on Wednesday. There were five of us: the gym teacher, the arts and crafts teacher, the cooking teacher, Elli Stehr (a girl from our class), and I. We started off at 2:00 and went first to Friedrichsbrunn. At first we had to walk our bikes for quite some distance, but then we had a lovely ride. At the children's home in Friedrichsbrunn we visited a former Thale student. The nurse who runs the home was extremely nice and served us coffee as soon as we arrived. From there we planned to go on to Treseburg to visit our people at the convalescent home. Just beyond Friedrichsbrunn, I suddenly hear "pffff..." and a loud bang, I get a huge shock, and what's happened? My rear tire has a huge hole and all the air has gone out. What to do? We had no tire cement, so at first I just kept cycling with a flat tire. Luckily we soon met a car that was carrying a bicycle with a side-bag of tools, and we asked the man whether he had any tire cement. He was terribly nice and immediately mended my tire properly. It was a delightful feeling to sit on an intact bike again.

This time I've managed to unpack all my news. Many warm greetings and a cheery little Whitsun kiss,

your Anni

Are you going to decorate the house with birch branches again? The chestnut tree here is blooming and blooming. I've also seen lilacs blooming already. Just imagine, the Youth Director class will take a field trip to Vienna. They will take the steamboat from Passau and return via Salzburg and Munich.

Treseburg, May 23, 1929

Dear Mama and Hilde,

First of all thank you very, very much for the loving Whitsun greeting, such a fine little package! Here is a little thank-you kiss for everything.

On Whitsunday early at 7:30 in the morning we went through the whole house singing. I spent most of the rest of the day reading and doing nothing in particular. Whitmonday was such a lovely day starting early in the morning. It was also quite warm. Emi-Margret and I took a beautiful morning walk. Later on there was an incessant stream of people out—once again, there was a total mass migration to the Bode Valley. Shortly before 3:00 one of the teachers came to tell us that we would be going to Treseburg on Tuesday and asked whether Emi-Margret, I, and another girl would like to go up already that evening. Naturally, we were thrilled and immediately agreed to go. So we packed our knapsacks and soon started off with beaming faces.

When we arrived we had to open up the house and wake it up. Then we immediately prepared a lovely supper and ate in great leisure. Next morning the weather was again beautiful. We got up shortly before 7:00, made a fire, and went into the garden to take our early exercise. After we had tidied up the house, we armed ourselves with deck chairs, blankets, pillows, straw hats, and books and stretched out in the sun. We lay thus for about two hours and were about to prepare our lunch when the others appeared. We had been quietly hoping that they wouldn't come at all since it was so pleasant to be just three. But now they had arrived and it turned out to be a lot of fun.

Our midday repast on the first day consisted of blueberry pancakes. The next day we had red cabbage with potato salad followed by sandwiches of pancakes and jam. Today we are having semolina pudding with melted, browned butter, cinnamon sugar, and gooseberries. Don't those sound like wonderful things? And they tasted accordingly delicious.

This morning started off with a lesson in educational theory and then we set off again from Treseburg with well-provisioned knapsacks. We spent the afternoon on the meadows by the Bode River again. If the weather is nice tomorrow, Frau Direktorin is planning to come up and we will visit a children's home in Stiege.

Is the pond open for swimming again? Did you have nice Whitsun days? I'm so glad the cabin has been fixed up again so nicely.

And now a very affectionate little kiss on the summer breezes from your

Anni

Thale, May 31, 1929

Dear Mama and Hilde,

Now we are back in Thale again. This morning early we set off with bag and baggage from Treseburg. Mama's last Sunday letter was brought out to me by somebody from Thale on Monday; it made me very happy. There were so many things to be glad about in it. It's wonderful that Reinhold got the position in Jena.

We continued to use the days in Treseburg to the full. On Saturday the art teacher was there. We had a drawing class early Saturday sitting in a meadow and drawing flowers. The day before we had scrubbed the house from top to bottom until it sparkled. On Sunday we took walks morning, afternoon, and evening. The weather was outstandingly beautiful. This was especially to be felt on the main road, which was packed with cars. They were even parked on the meadows by the Bode River and people were picnicking there. A fat policeman was also there; he gave them all tickets with great delight.

Monday morning early was a grand laundering. The big boiler was heated, the washtub rolled outside into the sun, and then we were out on our knees washing. I can assure you that it absolutely radiated whiteness (the laundry, I mean). By midday everything was hanging on the line, which was good, because just then Emi-Margret appeared with visitors from her home. They were on a trip with the older school children from the Sparhof and came to visit her, ten of them in all. We served them semolina pudding and then they rested for quite a while in the garden before hiking on.

Years later, Anni had a different perspective on this meal: "We were supposed to cook them lunch, and our best idea was to cook a big pot of semolina. We thought it was an enormous quantity. But they were hungry, and it seemed to disappear too quickly for them. Many years later I heard how the boys–including Emi-Margret's brother Heinrich–had all but starved on the amounts we thought would fill them up. But they were very polite and did not give any hint at all."

Now all of us in Thale are preparing for Frau Direktorin's birthday, which will be celebrated next Wednesday. It will be a sort of Treseburg folk festival, with every class preparing something. We are brooding ceaselessly over the plans. This afternoon we practiced songs and rounds which we will sing to Frau Direktorin early in the morning. We will be presenting her with a gift from all of us as well.

So now goodbye–I am sending you a lovely fat Sunday kiss,

your Anni

Thale, June 7, 1929

Dear Mama and Hilde,

Here is a little kiss for your loving Sunday letter. This week seems endless, probably on account of Frau Direktorin's birthday. Last Sunday we did nothing but compose, rehearse, and plan, but in the end we accomplished it and had a great success with our play. It was called *Therese's Legacy* and took place in the villa at Treseburg. We based it on a Treseburg legend and added all sorts of incidents that happened during our stay there. Parts of it were quite spooky. Ghosts appeared! Emi-Margret fainted and I almost succumbed. I was Emi-Margret's nurse and chambermaid and looked very old and worthy.

This is how the day went: At 7:00 in the morning we sang "Lift thine eyes" in three-part harmony outside Frau Direktorin's bedroom door. The evening before we had made everything beautiful in the red room and veranda, and had set the table and decorated it with flowers and greenery. It looked very cheerful. At eight o'clock she was fetched from her room while we all stood in formation along the hall up to the veranda, each holding a colorful balloon or flag. We also sang a funny round. Then she was presented with her gifts downstairs and afterwards we all had a very nice breakfast together. Nothing particular happened during the morning, except that everything had to be prepared for the afternoon and evening. At 3:30 p.m. the birthday events continued. First came the Hort children to wish Frau Direktorin a happy birthday. Then everybody had coffee together in the white hall. There was a huge array of pastries set up in a horseshoe shape. Then came the daycare children, ages two to six. They were all wearing garlands and looked terribly sweet. Altogether there were about two hundred people there.

Then came the presentations. First was the circus. The Hort children participated in this and did terribly well. All kinds of other amusements followed, including fair games such as target practice and a wheel of fortune where you could win marvellous prizes. We had an early supper at 6:30; the children had already gone home before that. Our play was at eight o'clock, followed by a presentation by the charity school and then another play, *Peter Squenz,* which was performed by the senior girls.

The presentations were all over around 10:00. Then we still did some dances and even had the ice-cream wagon come with the two attendant ice-cream men. Then there was a closing dance and we sang an evening round together, and thus ended the day. Of course we had to clean up afterwards but it didn't take all that long. In any case it was a very nice day.

Next Sunday we are going to Berlin. I have enough money for that–we need around 35 Marks, which I have. Do you think I could ask the Wächter relations if I could stay with them, or should I rather go to a youth hostel? Please let me know as soon as possible. I couldn't write you earlier about this because we ourselves weren't sure if the trip would happen. It may be that we'll go straight from Berlin to our practical work assignments. At the end of next week we'll still have a three day singing course, similar to the one in winter, but this time one of Jöde's colleagues is coming. I'm looking forward to it very much.

Is Reinhold working already? The tulip is blooming unwithered on my dresser. Please answer soon! And now, here is an affectionate little kiss for Sunday from

your Anni

4.

"Youth means being gripped by the infinite"

Anni left Thale as soon as the academic year ended. After participating in a Youth Movement "singing course" she traveled to Berlin to attend an international women's convention on social issues. Her next destination was the little village of Gettenbach, where she had been assigned to student-teach at a children's convalescent home. Germany's cities were still struggling to recover from the First World War, and many children who suffered from poor nutrition and other diseases of poverty were prescribed cure treatments in country institutions. The one in Gettenbach was picturesquely situated in a large manor house. Anni's weekly letters home continued throughout the weeks she spent there.

Gettenbach, July 5, 1929

Dearest Mama and Hilde,

 Your loving parcel arrived most punctually, thank you

many times for the long letter and the money. Now I have been here for a whole week and feel very much at home. I am not with the boys anymore but with the little ones, that is thirteen children from one-and-a-half years through seven years, so it's infants and older children. The two littlest, two and one-and-a-half years, can't walk yet but they crawl around the whole room quite rapidly and get into all kinds of mischief.

Living together in the house here is very enjoyable. There are seven "aunties," the matron, one nurse, and then the cook and various kitchen-maids and house-maids, a chauffeur (a la Rosenberger), and an elderly handyman. The matron left on Tuesday and probably won't return while I am still here. She went to attend a Fröbel conference and will take her vacation right after that. She is extremely energetic and everything always has to be spic and span, but she is very nice.

There are three of us in our section–a kindergarten teacher, a so-called "house girl" (that is, a girl from the local elementary school), and I. Of course it's a lot of work because of the children's circumstances, but they are such enchanting little people that it's really a lot of fun. Every day there is something new to be experienced, often the funniest little things. Especially the two littlest ones are terrifically sweet. These children will stay until July 18, and then a new group will come for a course of convalescence. I'm very happy that I will experience another group, since there are so many things you can learn. At the same time it will be sad when all these dear children leave us to return to their old and often bleak circumstances.

Hopefully everything is still going well in Keilhau. I'm sending you an affectionate little Sunday kiss,

your Anni

Are you also canning now? Here a lot is being canned – cherries, gooseberries, and strawberries.

Gettenbach, July 12, 1929

Dear Mameli and Hilde,

When the mail was fetched last Saturday I could hardly believe at first that the enormous package was for me. Now I am abundantly provided for with everything. And you always tuck such lovely things in between. You are so extravagant with me! Thank you so much for everything.

Last Sunday was very nice. In the morning we played happily with the children and I had the afternoon off. I really enjoyed that. The car was just driving to the station to drop someone off who was going to Gelnhausen, so I went along. That was fun and on the way I saw something of the area. Gelnhausen is a market town with a very lovely old church and several different pretty corners. The area is really very varied: fields and villages alternating with woods and mountains.

When we were back home I first wrote some letters, read, and took a nice walk. The afternoon had just turned nice, earlier the weather was quite unfriendly and rainy, but in the afternoon it brightened up although it remained cool. Since yesterday and the day before we've had proper summer heat.

The children are outdoors the whole day, also eating and sleeping outside at midday. The days go by very quickly. Next week on Wednesday the children are already leaving again. That is the end of their convalescence. In between there will be five days' gap during which there will be a great housecleaning. And then the new children will come. A couple of the current children will stay, especially the ones that are in special need of recovery and have gotten an additional prescription.

I've just gotten a definite answer from Thale. My practical work will last until August 8 and I have vacation until September 15. On September 16, I start again at Thale.

The matron, Marianne, has a birthday on August 9. I may stay for that. She was in Munich at a Fröbel conference and just came back on Wednesday and told us lots of interesting things about it, particularly about the kindergartens and convalescence homes in Bavaria which in general are a little behind the times.

I'm not surprised that you can't find Gettenbach on the map. It is a tiny village, no bigger than Keilhau. It is a little to the north-east of Gelnhausen which is near Hanau.

Have you been swimming in the pond yet, Mama? I'm looking forward to that like crazy when I get home. Hopefully the weather will be cooperative then. Are you busy with canning? Here in some places the wheat fields are being mowed, which already looks a bit like fall.

Many greetings to Reinhold from me. And for you a most affectionate Sunday kiss from your

Anni

What did Reinhold tell?

The summer ended, and Anni, after spending a few weeks in Keilhau, returned to college in Thale. Outwardly, her life as a student continued in its accustomed course, and she continued to write home with lively descriptions of college events.

Thale, October 5, 1929

You dear good Mama and Hilde,

Tuesday we had a very nice day in the daycare. Two students are leaving for good, so we celebrated with the children from both the daycare and Hort groups. The Hort children had made apple cake and set everything up beautifully, so that the whole thing was very festive. After we had eaten, the older children did a couple little performances and then we played circle games with everyone until the end. That was the last afternoon in the daycare for now. Since then we've mainly had theory and technique. Actually a new student teacher has arrived for the daycare, one of the Hort teachers who has just passed her exam. Now she first needs time alone to work herself into things.

For the moment Hort is closed, because the school children have fall vacation and only a very few were coming. As soon as more come we will start working in Hort again. I'm very happy that we are having some theory now. By the way, yesterday we got our notorious fairy tale papers back (we had handed them in on May 1). I got an A, Emi-Margret also got a good mark. But our two papers are very different. We are now being stuffed with civilization and natural history, three times a week, a two-hour class each time. We have a different teacher now, and I think the classes are better. The exam for this subject is very demanding. We are now thinking frequently about the exams. Now we get to be the "senior Hort students" for a whole year.

Now that we don't have practical work anymore, we have a lot more time to read and in general to pursue our own interests.

In the last few days there were a couple of huge storms with strong rain, but now it's beautiful and warm again. The fall colors are magnificent, but it's going terrifically fast. Tomorrow, on Sunday, we will definitely go on a nice walk. You too? I wish you a wonderful Sunday and send a most affectionate little Sunday kiss,

your Anni

D I A R Y

November 10, 1929

It is so strange as a young person to find out about yourself from books. But that knowledge recedes in the face of reality, because then you behave the way you are expected to. I would just like to know whether it's really different for mature people than for us—I mean those people who really stand for something and who don't simply exist. It must be strange to have a world-view. I don't think that we would even want one—we only trundle along in our doubts and muddle through.

And that is how so many are; we also have no ideals. The will to make something of oneself is also much less strong than it was before. Maybe the only benefit is that one doesn't deceive oneself so much anymore. The only things that remain sure are the people to whom you believe you have found even somewhat of an inner relationship. That's why it is so upsetting when you can't reach people, when no connecting points develop. There are only a very few such people, maybe two or three, and the rest basically don't concern you.

A book remains a book and there are so many of them, each saying something different; none can become sacred to me. That is why it causes me almost physical pain not to dare to approach the person who means something to me. I don't want to discuss any profound problems, I don't want to make myself interesting, I simply want to be near that person and talk quietly about ordinary things or nice things, or be completely silent; only to know that next to me is a person who means something to me. But of course it is presumptuous to require even that much of another, for only I need that person; the other (Kühn) does not need me. If one only knows that such a person exists, life becomes exciting, alluring, spurred on, and productive. A book, however, is not a person, it is something removed and distant. It can't summon up such heightened feelings, as only certain people can. For the sake of a person you can believe something, otherwise not. What does believing and not believing mean anyway? What is religion, and who has it? Where do great people get their beliefs from, their conviction? Have they had an experience of God? Something like that must doubtless have happened to Gogarten, but how can he speak like this, and why? Tillich says, "Youth means being gripped by the infinite, and therefore youth is religion." Who is it that is gripped? We can't believe anything anymore, because we know too much. Everything has its name and is classified and arranged neatly into its place.

Of course people say that to be eternally seeking and not finding means an incomplete development, but to me it still seems the best option. Who can dare commit himself to a certain course for the whole length of life and declare a certain conduct of life to be self-determining and binding? Or does having a certain view of life mean the same as having a profession: sacrifice and constraint? I would think it should mean fulfillment.

At times these questions are so distressing and pressing, and later you could say that the crisis has passed, but the conflict is not resolved, it is just repressed and numbed, and the worst of it is that then there is a great emptiness since neither the fulfillment nor the question is present. And these times are almost worse than the time of fear—yes, it is empty and dull and meaningless. Then I try to learn and read and to master new systems until it all breaks down again.

For some time I thought I shouldn't write anything about myself, since I can't formulate it and it would only annoy me later. But now I am writing this here, because I will want to know how it was. Why should one always swallow everything, why do I make myself into a secret chamber from myself? What I have written here is of course not for others – it has no form or central theme. It is disconnected and disorganized, just as it was inside me and how it came out. I could also copy my paper on fairy tales here; it accidentally turned out as it did and says more than I wanted to.

As their friendship continued, Emi-Margret lent Anni several books published by her community's publishing house, including some written by her father. Eberhard Arnold had earned a doctorate in philosophy before leaving academia to found a life of practical brotherhood, and he wrote forcefully about the importance of putting one's ideals into daily expression. Anni returned the books without comment; they posed the same questions that she was not yet willing to answer. Later she had occasion to meet Dr. Arnold when he visited his daughter at the Thale college. A well-known public speaker, he was asked to address the student body, and spoke to them about the aims of the community at the Sparhof in a manner that affirmed the goals of the college. At the end of his talk, he reminded the students that the Sparhof community had taken in numerous abandoned children and requested any of them to "come to us for a year and share with us in giving these children a home." Anni did not seriously consider taking him up on his request. Her overriding reaction to Dr. Arnold was one of awestruck respect, and his purposeful manner made her feel "very, very young." Emi-Margret's aunt Else von Hollander, a single woman who was a co-founder of the community, also visited the college. Anni was attracted to her serious, yet kind and natural demeanor, and they spent a long evening talking in the girls' room. But Anni shied away from too close a connection to Emi-Margret's community.

Anni said nothing about her inner struggle to her mother, who she knew was working hard just to keep the Keilhau school running. With Hilde's health continuing to decline and both Anni and Reinhold occupied with their studies, Frau Wächter had too much to do and looked forward to the day when her son and daughter would return home to help her with the administration of the school whose identity was so closely tied to that of the Wächter family.

Thale, November 15, 1929

My dear good Mama,

For Sunday I am sending you a specially affectionate greeting. Last Sunday I had lots of mail. The letter you and Hilde sent from Keilhau came, as well as a separate one from Hilde.

Last Sunday nothing particular happened. We had a tranquil day at home. This Sunday evening there is a Walter-von-der-Vogelweide celebration, namely, a remembrance day for the seven hundredth anniversary of his death. In the small choir we are singing a very beautiful pilgrim's song. Someone will make a speech about him, his poems will be read, and the voice teacher will also sing one of his songs. It should be quite nice. In addition we are currently practicing a very old Christmas cantata for two vocal parts, two violins, and piano in the small choir. It sounds wonderful. We will sing it early in the morning of the first Sunday of Advent.

We are all looking forward terrifically to the first of Advent, of course particularly the older ones since the younger girls have no idea yet about how it is celebrated here. Yesterday we fetched lots of fir branches for Advent wreaths and decorating, before it starts to get freezing cold.

Frau Direktorin Maria Keller believed that her students should learn not only to teach practical and academic skills, but also to help awaken a child's sense of awe for special and holy events. Because of this, the college celebrated the first of Advent in such a way that new students would themselves experience the start of the Christmas season as a time of mystery and joy. Emi-Margret later described how at midnight "three teachers went through the rooms of the college singing an old German song, 'From heaven high, bright angels, come!' In front of each door they left a small fir tree with lighted candles, apples, and cookies. New students knew nothing about this experience beforehand."

Now on Monday evenings we always have choir practice with the big choir and everybody comes. It is
highly necessary, since we only manage to sing a very
few morning and evening songs, and those badly. In
the coming days we'll definitely sing a lot of Christmas
songs. Mondays we are usually kept well occupied. Early
in the day we have active games for an hour and then
get ready for Hort until noon. From 2:00 until 6:30 is
Hort. At 6:30 there is a news report and then a lecture on
local history and geography, that is, one of the students
tells about her home town and shows slides of it. Then
there is a stand-up supper, which is a new invention for
days like this. We all go into the big hall, where a table is
set with platters of sandwiches and pots of tea. Everyone
helps themselves, then strolls here and there with their
supper until they have had enough and nothing more is
left. Of course this goes a lot faster than in the dining
room. At 8:00 we have choir until 9:30. Of course not
all days are packed this full, but sometimes it's fun to go
from one thing to another.

Yesterday evening we had to go to Stecklenberg, a
tiny village a good hour from Thale. There is an administrative center for youth homes, and they were having
a conference for youth directors and other members of
youth organizations. It was the last evening and we from
the college were supposed to present a play that we had
given there three weeks earlier. It was a comedy called
The Bear Knight. But the people were so stupid that
they didn't laugh once. In any case we did not perform
too gloriously, although it was dutifully applauded

afterwards. We however weren't at all put out but went home in high spirits. It was a beautiful moonlit walk and everything outside was quite bright.

Please Mama, you shouldn't wear yourself out and don't have any worries about Christmas. I'm sure everything will turn out beautifully. We will make it really relaxing and festive. I think our holidays will start on December 21 at noon. Now a very fat, affectionate Sunday kiss for you and Reinhold from your

Anni

Thale, November 28, 1929

My dear, dear Mama, and dear Reinhold,

I am sending you many greetings for the first of Advent, a whole package full and some Christmas spirit to go with it. You should light the candles, and Reinhold should play Christmas songs, and you shouldn't think only about housekeepers and lawyers. Watch out: I am thinking about you very much as you will soon notice.

Here in the house everything is very mysterious already. Three big wagons of greenery arrived and yesterday evening much was done in secret, until late. Some of the new girls noticed something and were very astonished that so late in the evening there was still a commotion in the house. Tomorrow, on Saturday, everything will be thoroughly cleaned and then we'll continue working for the bazaar, as is the usual custom.

There will be another parents' evening in two weeks at which we will celebrate Advent. In the Hort class the children are busily working on Christmas gifts for their parents. At times there is great sorrow when stitches have to be taken out and done over.

Now I want to put some serious thought into the question of how we can make Christmas really special. Unfortunately at the moment there isn't a lot of extra time for that.

I wish both of you a very beautiful, happy Advent Sunday – you should really make it like Christmas. If only you could be here, Mama, to see how beautiful everything is at Advent.

And now an affectionate kiss from your

Anni

You should put the little wreath on the table; the candles are meant to be stuck into the wreath (they are on pins that were heated and stuck into the candles). The peanuts and cookie hearts and oranges are for you to enjoy. *Guten Appetit!*

Hopefully everything arrives in good shape.

Anni celebrated Christmas in the Keilhau family home, surrounded by the traditions and values that were the constants in her life. Yet with the 1920s ending and her final months at college beginning, it seemed to her that the most fundamental parts of life were awash with questions. The following decade would change Germany beyond recognition and lead Anni to places more remote than even her imaginary childhood world of heroic knights and Indians.

5.

Last Months in Thale

Thale, January 19, 1930

It is oppressive to have to be spiritually dependent on people who actually mean nothing to you. One is and remains the teacher still in training, incompetent, ignorant, immature, "stuck in adolescence." To take your place as a human among humankind seems to me the hardest challenge. People are and remain in these official relationships to each other: teacher and student or this course and that course. Only for God's sake, don't bring up universal human questions such as art, literature, or philosophy. That is not at all the thing. Some people actually do it, but then they also always feel obliged to bare their whole heart, which is so embarrasing. Isn't it possible to ever converse in a purely objective, human way about such things? I feel here as if I am even more distant from the world and from life than during the deadening years in Naumburg. It's as if one is artificially preserved; there is nothing to be felt of the rhythm of time. The worst is the dependence, being deliberately kept within the kindergarten teacher milieu. Little doses of educational theory are administered to each according to what is felt best for this or that person. Things are now so dead, so lifeless – will it continue like this throughout the whole of life? Will there ever be a time when I can give all of myself away without consideration, even if afterward I recognize it to have been a mistake? At least it is good to have the unknown ahead, which leaves more possibilities open than if you have a world-view. How do you even begin to experience something of life? You have to search through everything, try everything, only have no fixed point, no position with retirement privileges. Are there any people left at all who fulfill a calling? It's certainly always the best if one can forget oneself.

D I A R Y

Thale, January 26, 1930

It's always good when someone occasionally arrives who isn't in the grip of the social conventions here. Jürgensen, the voice teacher, makes everything so absolutely original and lively. The longer I'm here the more the school seems to be a proper little women's republic whose atmosphere is almost stifling. All relationships are arranged in great objectivity, but then, repeatedly, disturbing personal conflicts arise. There is no clarity. "Only always beware that no one comes too close to another." In matters of religion, politics, or purely questions of viewpoint the rule is to be as indifferent as possible, the principle being, "Don't disturb things." On the other hand a certain relationship has somehow to be made, according to form, convention, etc. And then suddenly some type of common feeling is supposed to arise. That is why things so often go awry. I was closer to the people at the school in Naumburg than with those here in the college.

And although modern pedagogy, etc. is so thoroughly discussed, inner authority is missing and nothing is changed. To be sure the form and outward arrangements have been changed, but these have not been filled with new content. People do ask for opinions and allow one to do some things on one's own responsibility, but the final, highest authority is always withheld. And especially among women it would seem so very upsetting and in complete opposition to general principles if someone twenty years of age were to try to offer an opinion contrary to that of an experienced Youth Director or student social worker, for example. In this respect men are really more objective and evaluate an opinion based on its merits. At all events we here are viewed as still "grasping at development."

A person can only continue to develop if more is expected and demanded of him than he is able to do. Otherwise he comes to a standstill or even regresses or develops a feeling of inferiorty because nothing is entrusted to him. On the other hand you also can't demand that a person renounce himself or become something else, with other gifts and abilities, just as authority wishes. On the one hand too little is demanded and on the other, the humanly impossible.

The news that Fräulein Dr. Kühn intended to leave the Thale college for a teaching position elsewhere was a source of distress for Anni, who considered her one of the few adults with whom she could be completely candid. Dr. Kühn's classes on child psychology, with their Fröbel-inspired emphasis on respect for each child as an individual, were a highlight of the academic offerings at the college for both Anni and Emi-Margret. Dr. Kühn, who had also befriended the girls outside the classroom, was aware both of their friendship and of the differences between them. A Christian herself, she observed the contrast between Emi-Margret's childlike faith and Anni's agonized seeking. She also saw how Anni's outlook was affected by her friendship with Irmgard Blau, who continued to advocate a permanently questioning mental attitude. Dr. Kühn once remarked to Emi-Margret, "I wonder who will win in Anni's heart, Irmgard Blau or you?" "Not me, I'm too stupid," replied Emi-Margret, a year younger and less sophisticated than the others. "No," said Dr. Kühn. "It's deeper than that."

Anni's world was changing in other ways. As the years passed, the Youth Movement had become better organized, more given to ideological disputes than to disorganized celebrations in woods and meadows. The emphasis on the glory of youth was gradually replaced by an emphasis on the glory of Aryan youth as the National Socialists harnessed the energy of the Youth Movement for its own ends. On a personal level, a new note had entered Anni's friendship with Irmgard, who resented Emi-Margret's growing influence on Anni.

Meanwhile, with their final semester at college approaching, exams loomed for the Thale students.

Thale, January 31, 1930

Dear Mama,

My thanks for your last loving Sunday letter come in the form of a big Sunday kiss. Last Sunday was an excellent day, as you will have gathered from my birthday letter to Hilde. We had a wonderful musical evening, playing and singing together. Monday was a most eventful day in the Hort class, as I had to make cookies for the parents' evening with ten children. They enjoyed the process terrifically. First they looked on with great interest as I mixed the dough. The excitement rose to new heights when we reached the rolling and cutting-out stage. Now it was too thick, now too thin, now the dough was too sticky, now it crumbled, and from all sides arose cries for help. At the end it turned out well, some of the cookies were a little thick, but they were all tasty nonetheless.

We poor sufferers are plagued with work at the moment. For the Hygiene class we had to write a paper about all the glands in the human body. We wished that no one had ever been born with such a thing as a gland. It's a frightfully boring assignment, you just have to scrabble facts together from various books and then assemble them as deftly as you can. Hopefully this particular menace will be over tomorrow. And today in Educational Theory we had another paper sprung on us. In three quarters of an hour we had to describe the benefits and drawbacks of a country boarding school. It's a good topic, but sadly we couldn't do justice to it in the time allotted. Naturally we had just gotten into stride when we had to stop. The main point of the exercise was to be able to state clearly what we wanted to say and organize our ideas.

Now I have to stop, as it's already late and the others want to sleep. Warm greetings for Sunday to you and Reinhold.

Your Anni

Thale, February 28, 1930

Dear Mama,

Thank you for your loving Sunday letter. The newspaper clipping about the Friedrich Fröbel Center conference interested me very much.

Just think, tomorrow evening Irmgard Blau is coming from Halle for a visit until Sunday or possibly early Monday. Because one of the classes has gone to do practical work there is an empty room where we can live together. Won't that be nice? I'm looking forward to it very much.

The members of the small choir are planning something very beautiful for the middle of March. It will be an evening devoted to Mary. Our drawing teacher will show slides of Mary from the earliest pictures up through modern ones. During the slides we will sing songs about Mary, both old and contemporary. One especially beautiful song is Brahms' "Ave Maria." We sang it once at the Naumburg academy. There are also plans for an evening's entertainment to be open to the public. The big choir will sing various songs, some funny and some more solemn, mostly old folk songs in several parts. Interspersed between the songs will be rounds and instrumental music, possibly a comic musical play as well. Of course the hope is that many people will come and we will earn a lot of money.

And now many, many Sunday greetings and a fat Sunday kiss for Mama from your

Anni

Thale, June 20, 1930

Dear Mama and Hilde,

This time the Sunday letter will be short, as we are in the midst of affliction: it is to be noticed that the time of final exams is approaching. On Tuesday we had to write a paper for Health regarding the benefits of ocean and mountain climates. On Wednesday in Educational Theory we were unexpectedly assigned a paper about education in the Middle Ages. Today in Vocational Science we sat for two hours writing on, "How I would set up a daycare center for twenty children." Tomorrow we have a paper in Political Science, and on Monday in Introduction to Social Work. Then we'll have to do a paper on education and possibly another on Vocational Science. At the moment there are continual meetings and the provisional grades are being prepared. Wednesday afternoon and evening were most enjoyable. A flower competition was announced, the winner being whichever class could decorate a room the best. Three prizes were offered. And imagine, our class won first prize – isn't that nice? – consisting of a dinner with Frau Direktorin in the Forester's Lodge in Eckerode. In the evening the teachers organized a fête for us: we were invited to a "Fashion Tea." First we were regaled with tea and magnificent cakes, and then the teachers presented the latest fashions, including some really hilarious outfits. It was a priceless show and we laughed a terrific amount.

Thank you so very much for the dear Sunday letter and the very nice laundry package. The sweet little package of early fruits is delicious. The carnations arrived unharmed and we are all enjoying them. We are looking forward to Sunday, and with that an affectionate kiss from

your Anni

On Tuesday evening we had to exhibit our craft items, sewing, and art work. They were also graded. The stupid thing is that we won't be told anything about the grades.

D I A R Y

June 28, 1930

I never thought that things would be so bad with Kühn gone. I don't have an inner connection to anyone else. There is no inspiration, nothing is stirred up. The overarching connectedness with everything is increasingly lost.

I will always fight against the outlook that limits itself to asking how various things we learn will be of practical use to us down the road. It doesn't amount to anything that you know how to bathe a child. Those are just starting points; things which you simply learn. More to the point is, what would I do if I were suddenly a teacher at the Social Academy, that is, how would I grasp the whole connectedness of things? Do I know how our work fits into the whole of modern life? How it belongs into public life, to politics, the economy, and social conditions? What do I know of the condition and inner make-up of the people whose children are in my hands? How can I want to educate children when I have no idea of the essential nature or even existence of cultural values, when I am not attuned to the spirit of the time? People are educated with blinders on. Isn't it unbelievable that economics and social work are not official exam subjects but are lumped together under "business administration" and graded by a Youth Director with a purely practical background? By this one would be able to measure whether someone is prepared for the work; practical skills can always be acquired if someone has the will for it. This word "practical" reduces our whole education to nothing. The goals cannot be set high enough. The idealism so highly esteemed by the German Youth Movement has nothing to do with it; that is nothing but sentimentality; intangible, subjective feelings which no one even knows what to do with.

It is the same with this everlasting objectivity; there is nothing you can get hold of, it is cowardice. I don't want anything of objectivity or neutrality, I want opinion and counter-opinion. Which would give excitement to life. It's no wonder that people go to sleep, no wonder stagnations creeps in. This whole idea of neutrality is an illusion. The main thing is that a person does not become a high-handed egomaniac, but that they acknowledge the opposite opinion to their own personal outlook as in some way worthwhile. That is true objectivity: to be able to conquer your own self enough that you can acknowledge what is right, and then to fight for that with your whole inner arsenal. No one grows through neutrality; the only result is insipidity and nonsensical philosophizing. It just makes you stupid. This is also not what Kerchensteiner means by objectivity—he is for passionate personal involvement. If someone dares something, he can gain something. I am intentionally putting it crassly so that people will not think I am in favor of this kind of half-and-half neutrality.

It is also very hard knowing that there isn't anybody with whom you can discuss difficulties, someone who would simply listen and understand properly. A person you could look up to. It is so difficult to find such a one and then to build a relationship to them. I don't know if it's the same for others. To have such a person is definitely a necessity. This type of inner loneliness is the worst thing there is. Sometimes it could kill you. Conflicts and difficult situations can never be resolved, you just drag them around with you. But it could only be people with whom you feel an inner kinship. It cannot be just anybody. If only there could be something like that! It is also very difficult to find such a connection with another person. This can be very hard. The more complex a person is, the more difficult it is likely to be.

Why can't one simply get close to people – Horner, or even Kühn? But that is something quite different. It is unbearable that Kühn isn't here anymore, that we are taught by such a boring person as Schröder. Kühn is the person who up till now has meant the most for my life. This is not just an emotional enthusiam or anything like that. It is just how it is, and it is often bitterly hard.

I can see that my whole life is already botched, that it hasn't meant anything, that it was simply the life of a creature who was tormenting herself. All seeming success or recognition is only deception. At the bottom of my heart I never believed in it and I also dare not. It is self-deception when I believe, in happy moments, that I have been called to something. In reality it certainly is not so, I will never be able to do anything proper, neither practical nor theoretical. The worst is that I and others keep glossing it over, never wanting to speak the truth to anyone's face. And then everything falls apart and is very painful, but once it has, at least you no longer have any right to such presumptuousness. Sometimes self-contempt and repulsion with yourself take hold, and still the farce continues to be acted out.

This probably sounds very childish and unpolished but I can't help myself – it hasn't become any different in all the past years. And it's hardly likely it will ever change.

Thale, July 4, 1930

Dear Mama and Hilde,

This time I have truly excellent news to write. So first of all the best: another girl from my class and I were asked whether we would like to accept positions in fall in Gettenbach as assistant teachers. This is the same children's home near Frankfurt where I spent six weeks last year. Naturally we agreed immediately and already mailed our applications today. It was quite rushed and we will probably have to start there on September 15. That still leaves four weeks that I can spend with you. I am very happy that I will be going there, and particularly that there will be two of us. Of course I can't say how long I'll end up staying there. But isn't that good news? It came as a great surprise to me.

Last week we got our Economics papers back. Mine was the best, which pleased me very much. I'm going to take it as my optional subject for the exam; Emi-Margret is doing the same.

To wish you all a wonderful Sunday, here comes a little kiss,

your Anni

You naughty Mama, of course you sent much too much money. So just wait until I earn my own salary!

You shouldn't think I've run out of ink. It's just that at the moment I can't find my fountain pen.

Irmgard Blau visited Anni again toward the end of June. While they were together, Anni herself realized that the question Dr. Kühn had put to Emi-Margret – "Who will win in Anni's heart?" – would have to be answered. She attempted to wrestle her way through to an answer by outlining her thoughts in a letter.

Thale, July 4, 1930

Dear Irmgard,

You know, I actually wanted to write you a letter the other day before you left. Nothing came of it though. That is to say, I also soon realized that it suddenly didn't work any longer, that we two didn't know what to do with each other, and I was a bit afraid of Sunday. Can you imagine, I also wasn't able to clearly explain the dynamic here to you. It simply didn't work, and then you were there with the others. I couldn't reconcile the two things. Also, you are much better established there than I am here – you know the people in your group and there is immediacy in your relationship to them. Here the group is very different. I personally can't approve of the spirit or the way they do things, and yet I have to acknowledge that there is value in the whole thing, in its own way, and that I am dependent on it. But it is true, I really don't belong to this group and have no connection to the people themelves; they really don't concern me, with the exception of a very few. Yet I also don't have a proper relationship to your group, except perhaps through you, and that remains one-sided. Sometimes one doesn't rightly know what to do and feels completely at sea.

And then there's you and Emi-Margret – one certainly can't bring you together either. I have been eternally turning over in my mind how it is, when someone is part of a certain circle from the beginning (even if this circle continues to be open to others), by being born into it. Or if they first allow themselves to enter it a little, what happens, if they prefer saying yes rather than no to every new thing they encounter in the hope of finding a piece of wisdom in everything. For all its freedom of approach, this does have somewhat of a method and a purpose. If someone grows up in such a circle from childhood on, an unimaginable number of things are awakened and developed. Because of this some things are simply absorbed which others only discover much, much later with great difficulties and effort. And the resulting superiority, which neither can avoid, is continually to be felt. But then again, this life in an established circle sometimes makes things too easy, one is established there too easily, with too little trouble. The lifestyle is more grown into than struggled for.

There is a second way, which one could perhaps have more contol over, be more capable of changing, and possibly be less prejudiced in. One can easily become satisfied with something, only to throw it out again because of unwillingness to be committed, to find a center. Perhaps one wants to extend this searching around too long, spending too much time in opposition and seeking for something new and positive. It is possible that one is too dependent on the spirit of the times, and makes compromises and concessions more easily. What should one do with these two ways? I certainly don't know, and it's not all that easy to have to say yes to both and acknowledge both as equal and at the same time not to know myself what I should actually do in regards to it all.

I don't know if you can envision this completely. I believe that ever since the first time you were in Halle you've belonged to a group of people who acted in this second way. As time passed this crystalized even further and—despite the constant questioning—having such a connection to others must give you a certain sense of security. That's how it was for me. For quite a while I, through you, belonged firmly to it as well. Now I have encountered another circle. Although it cannot supplant the first, the spirit of your group is no longer so strong that it can prevail in me. I don't know what to do. I have explained this all somewhat schematically because I don't know a better way to explain it to you. I am not so much concerned with the question of how things are at the moment as with how it will be when I am finished with the exams. And to say it honestly, I don't know whether we two will be able to work together in the future.

I just want to write you frankly what has already been going through my head for a long time. At times this kind of thing comes pressing in, and at other times it is replaced by other things. The fact that we two lived together for so long in Naumburg had a great influence on me, probably more on me than on you. I was stepping for the first time into something in which you had long been active, the Youth Movement, or whatever you want to call it. You were really actively involved, in it with heart and soul. I was more of an observer; I sympathized with it and could sympathize with it because I regarded it as right. But I never really stood on my own in the midst of it. You were the active part; I went along with you. (All this doesn't have anything at all to do with the fact that it was a wonderful time. It is also not meant as an accusation against you; it is simply the situation as it appears from my perhaps quite one-sided point of view.)

I then presumed too much and came to think that I had actually arrived at all these things on my own, that I myself had had the initiative, had thought and acted independently, etc. And often, especially when I was on my own here in Thale, I imagined that you might also have thought that way and credited me with being more than I actually was. That's how it always seemed and that's how I also viewed it. But actually I always knew that the whole thing was a fraud, that I had been dishonest, that it was a presumption and an impudence, in which there was continually a false note. What's bad is that I, especially here, encouraged others as well as myself in thinking this, and you encouraged me in this. But I actually always knew (especially of you) that you actually didn't believe it, even when you said I would be able to stand on my own. I'd love to know whether you really did think like that, and why you did.

I myself actually don't know how I stand now, what is happening, and above all, what will happen. I know exactly how dependent I have been on you and it is so embarrassing to have to realize that again and again. Which is exactly why I preferred not to have to realize it. You obviously want to bring me back into the old group again. Why you care about it I don't know. But I also don't know whether I have the right to return. I believe in it less and less. But it is also very difficult to completely abandon it and that is perhaps the worst thing—not to ever really know, and yet despite all wishes to the contrary to have to come to the clear decision that it no longer comes into question for me personally.

You can imagine that this shillyshallying is not very heartening, and that it especially makes it difficult to meet new people and build a relationship to them. It is so difficult to decide, that is, to be honest with oneself. And when I think that we were intending to work together in fall, it may be that I was wishing to see things differently than they are because they seem so much more tempting and attractive that way. I don't think I can resist this. I don't know whether I should say yes or no. I think you will be able to find your way through this disorder. Please be completely frank. It wouldn't make sense to try to build on something that is meaningless. It took a long time for me to write this to you, but for once it finally has to be resolved. It is so difficult to clearly state something like this and I thought about many things that belong to it and which I thought I had written about, only to find now that I actually haven't.

Anni

The day after writing this letter, Anni left Thale for a class trip to Dresden which provided both a change of scene and a reminder that her Fröbel ancestry and the Keilhau school were a worthy heritage.

Dresden, July 7, 1930

Dear Mama and Hilde,

This is our third day in Dresden and already we've experienced a lot. The trip was just appallingly hot, I think the hottest day yet. Most of us (including me) are living at the charity school in Hellerau. Hellerau is a suburb of Dresden; it is a forty-five minute ride by streetcar. On this ride we promptly had our first adventure. The sky had already been completely black and dark brown, and suddenly a fearful storm broke loose. Dust was whipped up, so that you literally couldn't see a step in front of you and wave after wave of thick dust covered you. The trees were bent deeply over and we were worried that the little bus shelter would be torn away. It was a raging storm such as I've never experienced before. Later it started to rain very hard, and late that night there was a heavy thunderstorm. The streetcars couldn't run because trees had fallen on the tracks. Trees were uprooted all over and huge branches were broken off. At Vogelschiess Square many buildings collapsed and two people were killed. The whole thing is supposed to have been a tornado that originated in Spain and went all across Germany. You've probably heard about it too.

When we arrived here we longed for a thorough wash, and then we discovered something marvellous: a wonderful private shower arrangement. So every morning and evening we take full advantage of it. We're sleeping on straw mattresses in a high-ceilinged room that is used for gymnastics. It's tons of fun. The building is very big and beautiful, arranged very spaciously. Earlier it belonged to the Dalcroze Dance Academy. Architecturally it is very beautiful. The colors are very bright and harmonious, predominantly white and red. Only, some parts aren't very practically built so that many rooms can't be used at all, many big halls that used to be for gymnastics practice. In one wing there's a school for kindergarten and Hort teachers, a school for childcare workers, and a kindergarten. The kindergarten is set up terribly nicely. It is supervised by one of the senior girls that I know from Thale. Hellerau is way out in the woods, a kind of settlement with very pretty little houses.

On Sunday we had the day to ourselves. We could look around the city and anything else we felt like. First we visited all the notable places: the Zwinger Palace and courtyard, and the Brühlsche Terrace, and so on—all inspiring to see. Dresden is really beautiful. At eleven o'clock we went to the Catholic royal cathedral right next to the castle for high mass. Considering that it is in the baroque style, it is very simple inside, but that makes it all the more impressive. We went mostly on account of the choir, which is very famous for its motets, and the music really was extremely lovely. The church was crowded since it is famous for that.

Afterwards we visited the art gallery. Unfortunately there were a lot of people there and we were rather tired. I mostly looked at the *Sistine Madonna.* Altogether there are very many beautiful pictures there. We couldn't get around to all of them but we want to go again. Then we want to go to a special exhibition of Dresden artists. I would also like to visit the Albertinum where there are fine sculptures. We also went to see the Church of the Holy Cross.

On Sunday afternoon we took the steamboat to the king's country estate at Pillnitz. It took us about an hour and forty-five minutes to get there and it was a glorious trip past the White Stag. It was fairly lively and an unbelieveable number of people were swimming in the Elbe, then in addition paddle and rowing and sailboats in great numbers. It was very lively and colorful. Pillnitz was a pleasure estate of August the Strong. A huge flight of stairs goes right down into the Elbe, where he used to arrive with his gondola. The buildings are simple but beautifully arranged with lovely courtyards in between. On the return journey in the evening the lights on the river were wonderful. There are four bridges over the Elbe and through the various arches you could see the lights reflected in the water.

The day made us quite tired but satisfied. On Monday
we spent the whole day at the Health Exhibition. It is
an enormous building complex on both sides of a street
near the Dresden royal park. The buildings are all in
modern style, and mostly completely white on the
outside. Architecturally everything is extraordinarily
beautiful. The famous Kugelhaus is there also, but I liked
that less. A real little railway train with a steam engine
runs through the whole exhibition. As you go through
the various buildings there is a colossal amount to see,
and it's impossible to look closely at everything. We
took the whole day just to get around once. The exhibition is divided into sections: food, personal hygiene,
dress, public health services in various countries, physical
education, women and children, an international building
where the foreign nations have their exhibits, settle-
ments, farming, and much else. The Museum of Hygiene
is also part of it, but that is permanent. There's something
truly wonderful there – a human figure that is completely
transparent so that you can see all the veins and arteries,
the skeleton, organs, the brain etc. The various parts are
clearly labeled and are illuminated in turn. One can really
learn a lot from it.

Now I have to tell you something else: there is a
section where quotations of Fröbel are on the wall. And
there are pictures of Thuringia and one of Keilhau, of the
school, the famous photo of the entrance gate with Uncle
Gottlieb, Papa, and several boys. I think I'm also on it.
It is displayed very much enlarged. That made me really

happy. And then there are many pictures of Blankenburg and objects from the kindergarten in the Fröbel House. I liked this section the best.

Today we visited several convalescent homes, also very nice. I will write to you about that next time. In the morning we are going to the area known as "Switzerland in Saxony," to Ottendorf, where there is a convalescent home for youth.

Now an affectionate kiss from your

Anni

The envelope looks somewhat shabby, it has certainly been through a lot. Warm regards to all!

Anni returned to Thale at the end of summer to complete her exams.

Thale, August 18, 1930

Dear Mama,

I passed! It was splendid! We all passed, and everyone is beaming. I think everything went well. We are happy and everyone is terribly nice to us.

I will probably get home late Wednesday evening. Hurrah!

Until then, your Anni

6.

Crossroads

After a summer vacation at Keilhau, Anni returned to the children's convalescent home in Gettenbach where she had enjoyed working the previous summer. Her letters to her family from this period were not kept. However, she had an extensive correspondence with Emi-Margret Arnold and other friends, and she kept drafts of these letters in her diary. From the letters, Emi-Margret was surprised to discover that Anni, who had thrived socially at college and excelled in both academic and practical work, was finding life at Gettenbach difficult. Anni later recounted:

It was a very disappointing experience. I was not able to develop a relationship to the director, and I was often reprimanded. All the staff lived at the school, so we were together day and night for weeks on end. But there was no common feeling between us. It was just miserable.

The uncongenial atmosphere of the Gettenbach home

was due in part to the political opinions of its director,
Fräulein Schulze. National Socialist thinking and atti-
tudes were beginning to take hold across Germany, and
she had subscribed to these ideas in the time since Anni
had worked there the previous summer. Anni felt out of
place and lost.

D I A R Y

April 3, 1931

It is almost a year since I wrote in here. And what has
happened since then? Much and nothing. It seems as if
the world has come to a standstill for me, or rather I have
come to a standstill and am one of those who have grown
old while the new generation has already developed
completely different ways of thinking. Why is that? It is
because of the weakening relationships with those of my
own age and with other people in general.

If I stop to consider what has been gained in this first
year of my working life, it is desperately little. With how
much enthusiasm and faith in the future did I finish my
big paper last August! In spite of everything, I stand by
it fully even now, but I no longer have any faith in it. All
theory seems to me senseless in the face of this reality.
This year at Gettenbach will always be a black spot. It is
no service either to the children or to the home. It is more
or less just earning money. How well I can understand it
that young people are disgusted with the career system to
the point of simply running away. Often enough I have
felt like that too.

During the spring of that year, Anni was invited by Emi-Margret to come and visit the Sparhof community, a mere thirty miles away. As she later recounted:

Because I was having a hard time as a student teacher in Gettenbach, I was happy to be able to go visit one weekend. Everything impressed me terrifically – the simplicity, straightforwardness, and joy in life were similar to what I had experienced in the Youth Movement.

I spent most of my time with the children. There was a warmth and joy and naturalness about them that impressed me – they were so different from the children at the Gettenbach home. The community was very poor at the time. The children did not have a sandbox, and Emi-Margret told me how much they would like to have one. So when I returned to Gettenbach I sent them some money for a sandbox and sand.

I was impressed by the Sparhof community, there is no doubt about it, but I was not impressed to the extent that I especially wanted to go and stay there. I did feel that there was something genuine in the atmosphere of the community, and that continued working in me.

After the visit, she wrote to Emi-Margret:

April 14, 1931

Dear Emi-Margret,
   I had already resolved to write this letter while I was still with you. Hopefully you will find your way through

it somewhat. It is horribly hard to put things into words, and especially deeply-held thoughts. And even so you will have to read most of it between the lines. I have a great horror of all emotional outpourings and public displays of the depths of the soul. So to be able to say something like this that is personal and yet objective is not so simple.

You may have wondered why I was completely quiet while I was with you all. But you can't say a lot when something overwhelms you completely. Hopefully you did notice that the community, and especially Sunday evening, made a great impression on me. I will just write straight out how it is. Hopefully I won't scare you too much.

Since the time in the Youth Movement when I had a sense of fulfillment from true fellowship between people, I had never again experienced anything like that. That is now quite a number of years ago. There was always a lot of talking and reading and chattering about it, especially at school, but no one believed in it. No one actually wanted it anymore. On the contrary, the more it was talked about, the more repugnant it became and the more it revolved around the individual. And in spite of all you told me about your community, I really didn't believe in it either. Unless you experience something in and amongst people, even the best books are of no avail.

By the way, it is the same in other respects, for instance with religious faith. You could ask me, what do you believe in, do you believe in God, in Christ, or in the good, or in anything else? To that I can only say, I don't

know. There could hardly be a more cowardly answer.
But it is factually so. I have always wondered how people
who really have something to say – like Buber or Tillich
or Gogarten – how they came to their experience of God.
They must have once been overwhelmed by it, in order
to be able to believe persistently and unconditionally.

And when you say so simply, "We believe in the
message Christ brings of the community of all people
in one spirit," and then you act accordingly. And it is
actual and living – there is no discussion or babbling, no
senseless philosophizing. This made me very happy. I
had really not believed anymore that there were people
who really believed in something and consequently felt
compelled to do it. It's all the same in the end whether you
believe in the divine in man or above man. It only matters
whether the belief is real, that it grips the whole person
and gives meaning to all of life. Of course you remember
how much I used to resist the idea of my beloved "fixed
point," as I liked to call it. (Think of Kühn's classes.)

Do you understand what I mean? If you don't believe
in anything, it would be terrible to commit yourself to
something. Life still wouldn't have any real significance.

You probably thought it was strange that I don't
have any plans for the near future and that I am stepping out into the world in such an indifferent way. If you
don't know the whys and wherefores of things, nothing
seems to be of any consequence. Studying education and
economics is a vague mist. What's the use of it? I would
enjoy getting carried away with pedagogical ideals, but
that is no life's calling. And who would it benefit if I wrote

97

a couple of treatises or researched something? Certainly not the child; at best the result would be a couple more little categories into which children could be conveniently divided. An educator? No again. Anyone who is not a born teacher can never learn to be one from books. I have a holy terror of anything abstract, as much as I also unfortunately have a weakness for it, as you well know. Well, up to now my whole theory has been a complete washout. And what besides? I truly don't know. But please don't think that I am about to raise my voice in lamentation and pity myself a little. It is only a somewhat unpleasant fact.

The last part of the time here won't be so difficult to bear now. I am already endlessly looking forward to the fall. I also won't let things affect me so much anymore. You really can't imagine how much good it did me to be with you all yesterday. Refreshment was definitely needed. Never in my life have I been so asleep as in the last six months–I had just about fallen into becoming bourgeois, which is not exactly a happy thought.

Anni

May 4, 1931

Dear Emi-Margret,

Now for the first time I can properly understand how strange the atmosphere in Thale must have been for you, with its insincerity and cowardly neutrality. It disappointed me too, but only because I had hoped for other things from Thale, not because I had already experienced something different. What I had seen until then in Naumburg, etc. was not one bit different and therefore it seemed best to us – I know that many others felt the same – of course you know Irmgard Blau – not to bind ourselves to anything, not to hope or believe in anything, and to put a question mark after everything.

All human endeavors to give life new meaning appeared dubious to us as well, all the more dubious the more we experienced a mere senseless day-to-day living and squandering of existence everywhere. In every new attempt we had the secret fear that in the end this idea would also prove to be a delusive hope, a wrong path, something that in its final goal was unclear and indefinite.

You can probably imagine that this way of thinking about things isn't shed so quickly once it has become second nature. So you will have to have patience if I misunderstand or miss the point of many things that seem obvious to you. The inner critic which until now has been in the background of everything has only ever reached the intellect and hasn't wanted to have anything to do with the rest of the person. So it will take a while until the whole person can be overwhelmed by something without this intellectual criticism being mounted as a defense. And a person can easily be deluded into thinking that he is completely gripped by something when actually only the intellect grasps it. Then the danger is that a person's intellect may accept new insights and discard the old ones as unusable, only later to realize that the whole thing was a mistake because he was not in it heart and soul. But if it should happen that the whole person is fully involved, there couldn't be any breaking off of the old, but only a continued building. There can also be no regret or disappointment over something that has been done, only hope for the future. I wonder if you understand what I mean by being patient. It is easier to recognize something than to let your whole self be over-whelmed by something, because that requires that you are very ready and very humble and make yourself very open.

Anni

After several months, Anni visited the Sparhof commu-nity again. She later told:

I had no understanding of the Christian basis of the community. I was a Protestant by birth, but inwardly the Christian faith had no meaning for me. On the contrary, I felt there was so much hypocrisy that I had turned against it. But while I was at the Sparhof there was a meeting which impressed me. I do not know what the meeting was about, but I can only say that something of the Holy Spirit was moving there. It gripped me, and I felt: I have to come back here! I have to stay here! There was some-thing true and real that I had not found anywhere else, not even in the Youth Movement.

At one of the next meetings, the circle of members felt that they all needed to begin anew together, to pledge themselves again to their commitment. After the evening meeting a fire was built in the middle of the community, and we all stood around it in a circle. Emi-Margret's father spoke with great fervor and conviction, saying, "We want to give our lives to Jesus and burn away like these logs. We want to commit ourselves anew for this fire, for this light, and for the truth, and as a sign reaffirming that, let each one throw his log into the fire." Somebody went around and gave a log or piece of wood to each one who stood in the circle. Everybody who wanted to renew their pledge to Jesus was to put his log on the fire. While this was happening we were also going to sing. Now I was really in a pinch. From all I had experienced in the one day I had been there, I felt very drawn. I actually felt that this was what I wanted, but I was not completely sure, and I thought, if I put my log into the fire now and commit myself, and then feel differently later, what shall I do? I did not know how to get out of this situation. So I quietly let the log slide down on the ground behind my back. I thought no one would see, but apparently some people had noticed; they probably looked to see what I was doing. But it all impressed me immensely. I felt such an atmosphere of fire and dedication and surrender that I was actually convinced that this was the right way for me, but I wasn't sure whether I could keep such a promise.

DIARY

June 26, 1931

What shall I write to Emi-Margret now? It has never been so difficult for me as now. I have also never felt such a distance between us as now, although I don't know anyone to whom I feel a stronger bond. It is anyways true that, although the people from the community receive you very warmly and naturally, they are in fact very distant and unattainable. This is probably because one is not so indifferent to them as to most others. When will I go to the Sparhof to stay? Nothing else seems important to me anymore. But I know that it will then be a matter of an either-or. I think they expect more of me than I can offer. Since spring I haven't moved one step forward.

Can I go this way? Again and again come the question and the doubt. "We have often experienced it, that someone is spoken to so directly by the Spirit that they act immediately and turn with all their strength to the new way that has been shown to them." I believe that I have in some way felt the Spirit, and yet I haven't found the courage to come to a decision. I feel embarrassed when people speak about the coming of and hope for God's Kingdom. I am ashamed of reading the Bible. I don't understand any of it – I mean, I am not able to believe in it.

The worst of it is publicly vindicating and justifying myself.

As the months went on, Anni found the working conditions at Gettenbach increasingly difficult. She gave notice and returned to Keilhau where she spent several months nursing her mother, who had fallen ill. Anni did not intend to stay at Keilhau. She had promised Emi-Margret that she would return to the Sparhof to work for a year in the community school and kindergarten. Anni hoped to be able to travel to the Sparhof by the end of July; Emi-

Margret, who was engaged to be married, had invited her
to come to her wedding which was planned for July 26.

Keilhau, July 2, 1931

Dear Emi-Margret,

Since I left you I have thought of the Sparhof a lot.
During the evening by the fire I felt very clearly how
strong your community is. But since then I have been
depressed by the thought that I didn't participate fully in
it all. Yet it was a great experience for me. I am repeatedly
thankful that I could visit you from Gettenbach that time.
While I was at Gettenbach (but not yet with you) I had
always kept secretly wondering whether what I wished
for might be found among you. But I never would have
thought that what I did find among you–true life and
reality–could exist. Through this experience, words like
community, service, loyalty, and faith have changed for me
from abstract concepts to undeniable living facts. When
I came back here, I was strongly aware of the contrast
between you and this completely bourgeois atmosphere.

I don't know if you can properly imagine the narrow-
ness and restrictiveness that dominate here because of
the whole point of view of utility and expedience. To
what end do people tear around and wear themselves
out? Not out of joy in their work or at least interest in it
(that is only a secondary consideration), also not so they
can possibly help others. That takes third place at best.

Rather, it is so that after several decades have passed they have the biggest possible savings account which can then be enjoyed in peace and personal comfort. Of course, this goal is seldom attained nowadays, but then life is also basically over once all the business and economizing cease.

Why do people take up a profession? So that they can later settle down in a safe, secure nest with a good income and comfortable pension. People get upset and become sick and old all because they have lost money and want it back. There simply is nothing else here. Incidentally, some emotions can also really be quite nice and pleasant. For instance if someone is interested in their work. Or if someone does something for one charity or another or occasionally makes someone else happy. Then you have a soothing feeling that you have done all that is humanly possible. But that is all. Of course I never noticed this as much as I do now.

It's certainly not so upsetting when you stand by as a spectator and merely observe it. It is only bad when you are drawn into it yourself by people who are dearest to you. Here at home, no one would understand how someone could prefer an occupation that entails long hours, brings in no money, and is seemingly thankless. This lack of understanding comes to a large extent from love. Oddly enough, parents usually want their children to have it much better than they – in plain English, to have a successful career. My mother has now planned that I should become a professor of education. This is an irreproachable, refined, respected, and probably well-paid

profession. She cannot comprehend why I categorically reject it. Of course it's also very hard for me to say
anything. Until now I have hardly told them anything
about the community. It's also something that would
be quite incomprehensible here. My mother hopes that
I will now help her by earning and saving as much as
possible until she, my siblings, and I are well provided
for. And that is the terrible thing–that I will have to let
her down in this. Since it can only be either the one or
the other.

I have sometimes thought of the meaning of the words,
"He who leaves father, mother, brother, sister, goods,
and possessions for his name's sake will inherit eternal
life." And I've also thought of what your father has said
repeatedly, that you must not delay in following because
you still have to settle this or that. This has become a
difficult question for me. Should someone make himself
free for discipleship by breaking off from everything that
obstructs him (the loss which he himself feels is part of
the cost) if through this he injures the love of others?
Doesn't he then take a great guilt upon himself? Basically,
everything parents do is motivated by love for their children. And now, when it has come time to return this love,
all their hope is turned to disappointment. And they will
see that they have been left alone. (Until now there has
always been the possibility of returning to my parents'
house. But I know that then it wouldn't be possible in
the same way anymore.) I think that you can roughly
imagine this, Emi-Margret. In spite of this, there's actually no longer any doubt in my mind that sooner or later

I will go the one way. Only the question comes again and again – how can I make it less difficult and loveless for the others?

Unfortunately I am not yet courageous enough to make a full decision. As things are now, it's a betrayal of both the one and the other.

I love to think of how it is with your children. In Gettenbach I always felt it was terrible that so many people could have an influence on the children. There was also a contest among the adults (even if unacknowledged) with each trying to prove that her own method was best. Amongst you though, just because many people have an influence on them, true freedom and security exist. On the one hand, I think their childhood lasts longer and is more intense, and on the other hand they are able and ready to comprehend abstract thoughts much earlier than other children.

In regard to politics everything is very strange here. Everyone who considers themselves to be someone lives and breathes National Socialism. There is an excitement and ardor as hardly ever before, sometimes even more among the women than the men. It's as if it were the final salvation, like a secret religion. To me it is all quite incomprehensible.

Anni

Frau Wächter had been looking forward to having Anni home after six years of schooling. She was distressed by the idea that her daughter would now spend a year working (without pay) at a distant and unknown commune and

wrote to Emi-Margret's father in an attempt to learn
more about this new venture.

Keilhau, near Rudolstadt, July 15, 1931

Dear Dr. Arnold,

My daughter Annemarie would like to work with
you in your community. Her visit there made a strong
impression on her. I appreciate your kindness in wanting
to take my daughter into your circle. As you may know,
her time in Gettenbach did not do her any good and did
not give her proper fulfillment, which she now hopes to
find amongst you. It will be very difficult for me once
again to let my child go so far away and I could only
do this with much anxiety. So you will understand that I
have several questions for you. How had you imagined
Annemarie's work? Will you and your esteemed wife
guide her work so that her strengths can be developed?
Annemarie needs to be supported and simultaneously
encouraged, since she tends to be somewhat phlegmatic.
Unfortunately she is quite closed and sensitive and it
is difficult for her to come out of herself. She does not
lack joy in her work, because she loves her profession.
Would Annemarie receive a little spending money for her
work? I am not in a position to be able to support her
financially. Will Annemarie have to commit herself for a
longer time? How do you arrange these matters?

My daughter was too shy to inquire about these things
during her visit there. Annemarie feels very drawn to
your daughter and has become very fond of her. My

daughter was very happy about the invitation to their wedding, but unfortunately she cannot participate in it because I can't bear to let her go just yet. When would you think that Annemarie could come to you? I would very much like to have her here with me until the end of August.

Thanking you most sincerely for your trouble,

Most respectfully,
Frau Hedwig Wächter

Emi-Margret's mother, Emmy, replied to this letter the following day, enclosing a note to Anni.

Sparhof, July 16, 1931

Most respected, honored Madam,

We thank you from our whole hearts for your kind letter of July 15. We are very happy that your dear daughter Annemarie would now like to join our circle in order to work with us, after already having spent two years with our daughter Emi-Margret in Thale. We are very much looking forward to welcoming Annemarie, and we are sorry that she will not be present for the wedding on July 26. Because Emi-Margret will then be spending several weeks on her honeymoon, the end of August would be a very convenient time for Annemarie to arrive. Emi-Margret is very much looking forward to having her friend here then. We are now suggesting that Annemarie should first spend a year becoming acquainted with our life here to see whether life in community appeals to her.

We all feel very fortunate and would not want to live in any other way. We are now thinking that Annemarie would work half the day with children, either in Hort or in the kindergarten, and the other half day in the kitchen, sewing, or something similar, so that she could acquaint herself with the wider communal work and understand the connections between the different departments. You have asked about spending money or other such. No one here receives spending money, rather everything is taken from the communal account—all essentials such as clothing, stamps, writing paper, sewing supplies, or supplies for any journeys that may be necessary. Here it is like being in a family setting, and Annemarie will be treated just like everyone else, which will make her feel at home. Please allow me to enclose a few lines to Annemarie herself.

With respectful greetings, also from my husband and our whole community,

Your
Emmy Arnold

Enclosed letter:

July 16, 1931

Dear Annemarie,

Your mother's letter made us very happy today. We had always wondered whether we wouldn't hear from you soon. You can imagine how much we are looking forward to your coming and working here together with us. We think it would be good if you would have the chance to work in all areas of the community, but that will all fall into place once you are here. I understand you would most of all like to work with the children. It is too bad that you can't be here for Emi-Margret's wedding. We are already energetically preparing for it. Emi-Margret is still in Switzerland. We're expecting her back here by the beginning of next week. If you come as planned, she will be back from her honeymoon and will be able to acquaint you with everything herself. We are already looking forward to spending this winter together. It is so wonderful that everything we do here truly serves a cause that one can serve with all one's strength.

So please let us know as soon as possible when we may expect you.

Looking forward to working together this winter, both inwardly and outwardly,

Emmy Arnold
for the community

A few days later, Anni wrote to Emi-Margret.

Keilhau, July 21, 1931

Dear Emi-Margret,

You've most likely already heard that I am not coming for the 26th. I kept thinking it could be decided differently, which is why I waited so long to write. I am very sorry that it won't come off. I had looked forward so much to being able to be there then. Things aren't going well – it was difficult in the first place to reach an agreement and took quite a long time. And if I traveled now, there would be new difficulties and my mother would have more unnecessary worries, which I would like to try to avoid. This way she will have time to get used to it gradually. Until now I had always thought it could be arranged. But now I think it will be better if I stay here. I thought that I could then come around August 27 or 28, if that is all right with you. Will you be back home by then?

I am already looking forward to it so much. I hadn't known at all that my mother had written to you already. I knew she intended to but I thought she meant later. I thought that then she might be more reassured, since naturally she can't comprehend or imagine how things are amongst you. She worries about so many things which just don't bother me. But she did find your mother's letter very reassuring.

Your loving letter made me so happy. You sure know how to help me, dear Emi-Margret. The wedding invitations were so tastefully planned and beautifully written.

You are right when you say that it's likely a rift can't be avoided. I think the same. Otherwise it would be overly easy to slide from one thing into another. Perhaps then one also wouldn't be serious enough about it.

Concerning becoming a professor of education – that actually didn't cost me any deliberation. For one thing, as you said, after such an education I would be even more duty-bound to my mother. Besides which I would be completely incapable of teaching anything, which I hadn't properly considered until now. Please imagine me giving a lesson in pedagogy–it would be in all ways ridiculous. But the main reason is that nothing matters so much to me now as being able to come to you. (I know that even without that there are plenty of other things I could do.) There isn't any reason to be unhappy over it.

You were lucky to have just been in Switzerland. I recently read that you now have to pay an extra 100 DM to travel abroad. I'm glad you met so many nice people there. In that respect Keilhau leaves something to be desired. It's a bit boring. Books can't replace people, at least not as far as I'm concerned.

However, I am very happy with Fröbel's writings. You would also enjoy reading him. For him everything was life and action. He tried to live what he recognized. At any rate his life had meaning. Life in Keilhau in those days must have been very fine. I often had to think of you when I read. It was a life with a strong sense of community, which went along with inspiration and fulfillment. It was really a life that was dedicated to the future. I have already read various letters, diary entries, and essays, all closely connected with and based in the daily life in Keilhau. And I kept finding how things that are described in abstract terms in his *The Education of Man*–the meaning and basis of life described there–are actually confirmed in their everyday communal life. For example, I read reports about some of the students of that time, written in the form of a description of their character and development. There is such a serious exposition of the developing person, with all his potential and mistakes and good characteristics, that I can really believe everything he says in his book about character formation and education in its highest sense. And it always amazes me how new his ideas seem in relation to our time. You could easily imagine you were reading about the goals of the new boarding schools, for instance. Actually in the depths of my heart I had always thought that what he writes is all well and good, but it's just a theory among theories, and even if it is very illuminating, it probably couldn't become a practical reality. Now I've been completely proven wrong in that idea. What a shame that it's not like that here anymore. Maybe I'll write to Kühn about it once. She might be interested in it.

Please thank your mother for her kind letter to me. And please do write again once you're back home.

Anni

August 11, 1931

Dear Lilo,

I have given notice in Gettenbach. As time went on the work there became increasingly unbearable for me. Apart from the fact that it was physically strenuous, we were under such mental and emotional pressure that I simply couldn't stand it there any longer. This was due mainly to the manager, a Youth Director who was an exceptionally gifted person, both intellectually and as an educator. But she was conceited and self-confident to a degree bordering on sickness. She therefore couldn't tolerate any authority other than her own and kept everyone at an unapproachable distance from herself. As student teachers we anyways counted for nothing. She talked a great deal about herself and her achievements, and expected everyone to curry favor with her. When I first came, there was a sort of cult around her. She was considered to be practically infallible. This lessened later. I of course had no intention of participating in this, and was too stupid to do so anyway. But that was taken to mean that I was disloyal to the Home (which in a certain way was true although not what I had intended). In addition she had the habit of tyrannizing newcomers, especially student teachers; ultimately she had unlimited control over us and our time. Of course the work with the children was also disturbed because she claimed the sole management over them and no one else had a speck of authority.

Have you ever heard anymore from the Naumburg people? It's really sad that so many people vanish so quickly out of one's circle and you never hear from them again. If you don't say yes to something and invest yourself in it with everything you have, you will most probably always stand alone and grow away from other circles. Of course it isn't easy to find a circle of people that you can simply say yes to. But I believe that the community at the Sparhof could be one for me. The life there has made such a great impression on me. You know, I had never thought there could be something like that and therefore it surprised me and filled me to the depths. I can definitely say that since the year when we experienced the summer solstice celebration (June 23, 1926) I haven't come across anything else like it. You know, at that time we were really completely filled with it, despite the fact that outwardly in school and so on we acted quite mulishly. Life seemed to be so terrifically rich and worth living.

I believe, too, that those were the best days of our youth. For me at least it was the awakening and first awareness of myself and consciousness of the value of fully lived life. Do you remember? – We were overflowing with happiness. I still remember the summer evenings when we would sing in the Hosfeld's garden. Probably no one else could properly understand what that time meant for us. It belongs solely to the two of us. Because, if you think back on it objectively, it was a summer solstice celebration like many others, perhaps not even fully in the spirit of the Youth Movement, although we believed at the time that we had found the alpha and omega of the Youth Movement. But I don't think that harmed our youthful spirits at all. And I believe that since then a certain striving and seeking and feeling in us is no longer to be extinguished, even if it is sometimes expressed only in skepticism, hopelessness, weariness, and lack of faith. It would only take one spark to bring it all back to life. So I'm sure you will understand what the experience of the Sparhof community has meant to me.

Some time ago I read through our letters from the time of our great enthusiasms and even greater follies. However childish some things seem now, I wouldn't want it not to have happened. I think that at that time our development (and by that I mean, life) moved within us with giant strides. And so I have to write one more thing to you: though it often seems that life is pushing us apart and we don't really seem to know about each other anymore, there will always be one thing that will remain undestroyed between us, and that is the awareness of the deeply shared experience of that rich time in our lives. And I believe that this will help us in every difficulty.

Anni

Back in the familiarity of home, the experiences at the Sparhof grew distant, and Anni's promise to Emi-Margret to work in the community kindergarten did not seem like a pressing commitment. But teachers were needed at the growing Sparhof school, and after some months Emi-Margret wrote again urging Anni to come.

September 1, 1931

Dear Emi-Margret,

It was such a relief to get your letter. When I think of the letter that I wrote you and of the range of ideas I had at that time, I also have to say that the way you understood it was more or less correct. Although I would much rather be able to say that it wasn't so. Emi-Margret, you can't imagine how good it is that you wrote as you did. Now I hope that everything will come right.

In one sense I have to admit that the community had become far removed from me, not in its essence or the experience I had there, but more in space, as a personal reality, as if you and the people who know something of you were so much farther away. I have to say again, unreachably far away, as though I and others had become distracted with so many other things that the connection to you became weaker.

If only you can understand what I mean, if only it were possible to say it quite clearly. If only you don't have to think that the experiences I had there with you had been dulled or that the values that were shown to me while I was with you had become any less strong or less worth living for. If only you don't have to think that the things I wrote about in various letters were nothing but initial enthusiastic outbreaks, swiftly burning straw fires that expressed themselves in many fine words until they died out and made room for so-called common sense, and that therefore everything which was once wished for and spoken of was given up in favor of a creeping bourgeois mentality, that is, for the ease and indolence of a familiar lifestyle: it is my greatest worry that you might have had to think that. And I also have to say to myself that it must appear that way. I certainly can't deny that I do not singlemindedly and positively reject the middle-class spirit, however much I would like to leave it behind. One lives so much in the midst of it that it becomes almost instinctive. But quite apart from the straightforward path and the ease which are a natural part of such a life (and which often confine a person without their wanting or noticing it), I feel held back especially firmly just now on account of the events in my family. At that time you all seemed so far away from me that the worldview that was supposed to become self-evident to me here did indeed seem to be somewhat self-evident, and my steadfastness and will were not firm enough.

Dear Emi-Margret, please don't regard this and what I am still going to write as an attempt to excuse myself. Excuses often do nothing but raise one's opinion of oneself. I only want to describe how it was as best I can.

Oh, and that idea about my studies has become a bit of a problem. As you know, I had actually given it up completely. Then my brother came, and an uncle as well, and it was discussed all over again. And they talked and talked until I finally gave in and said that I would inquire with Kühn and so on. They wanted me to start right away on November 1. And although I'm very ashamed to admit it, I might almost have said yes to the idea. It's good that now it's completely out of the question.

But if I had started on November 1, I wouldn't have enjoyed it at all. When I wrote to you that I wanted more than anything else to come to you this winter, I wrote in the hope that once I was there things would turn out as they ought to, as you also wrote, and that everything else would somehow be solved. And that is also now my great hope, that once I'm with you, everything will be the way it should be. And it's not so important whether I'll perhaps study more at a later date; it's only important to me how it will turn out when I am finally there with you.

And again I'm afraid that you might think, because the question of my studies was raised and I had a certain joy in the thought of it, that I had on that account forgotten about all of you. My joy was not really that great (as I am just noticing now)–it was more my objective personal interest in it that caused me to respond with some enthusiasm. Please, don't think this whole business of studying is so important; it really is not. It is certainly not the goal of my life. My family set their hopes on it much more than I do myself. The only reason I wrote so much about it is to show you how it is all connected.

Your letter has brought the community very close and real to me again, which makes me very happy. I would really like to be able to write it–but I hardly dare to anymore and so will only keep thinking and hoping–that I will certainly come as soon as I'm not needed here anymore. It will still be quite a while until then, and it won't be possible before the end of October since my mother's recovery is so slow. It's very terrible for me to think that you are having trouble with the work because I didn't come in time. So I hope that things will be arranged here more quickly than seems possible now. For a while we were very worried about my mother but now we think the worst is over.

If I had had any idea of how it would all turn out here, I would certainly have come to your wedding for a few days. At the time I didn't want to come for just a few days because I dreaded the idea of having to leave you again. Now I can't come on account of the work here. And as much as I would love it if you could visit me here sometime and we could talk, the trip is too long and your work would have to be neglected. So I will just continue to really hope that it won't be too much longer until I can come. And if you can, dear Emi-Margret, write to me once in a while. I wish I could tell you how much I look forward to the time when my coming to you will be a reality. But I don't know if you will be able to believe that since I have only written about it so far.

Now once again I have written many words. And I would give so much if only a part of what I have written would become deed. It's very humiliating just to have to keep on writing.

Anni

Keilhau, November 22, 1931

Very respected, dear Frau Direktorin,

I have not written for so long that you probably had to wonder whether I had completely forgotten Thale. I have thought of Thale and of what it meant to me very often, and ask you to excuse my long silence and not to take it as ungratefulness. One always likes to write happy news, and because sometimes there's not that much happy news to write, it's a little hard to write anything.

At the moment I am still at home, but I don't know yet for how long; definitely I will stay here until Christmas. I actually wanted to start something else but it hasn't worked out until now because my mother fell ill in August and still has more recovering to do. There is a lot of work which is too much for my sister by herself. I had already made several different plans. First I wanted to visited Emi-Margret at the Sparhof and later possibly study pedagogy. But actually it's not the right time for me to start a course of studies. If and when anything will ever come of this plan I can't say at all. I just have to wait and see what will happen.

I was already very much looking forward to working with the Sparhof children. I visited the Sparhof two times from Gettenbach and I have to say that the life there left a deep impression on me. There is nothing of the wishy-washy unclarity of some of these reform endeavors and intentional communities, of which of course there are many. The people in the Sparhof have before their eyes a clearly defined, mighty idea for which they strive in firm conviction and for which they truly dedicate their whole lives. At the same time they do not overlook reality and world happenings. In every aspect of life they try, based on faith, to live out this idea. It's actually not surprising that such an attempt appears very strange. I left Gettenbach earlier than I actually should have because I originally intended to spend the summer at the Sparhof. And it was probably also good that I left Gettenbach. You have certainly heard nothing good about me from there. And rightly so. I am not trying to absolve myself or accuse anyone in Gettenbach in any way. Far from it. But I did want to tell you something about it. Sometimes people just don't get along with one another as one had originally imagined, and then that simply cannot be forced. You will certainly understand that difficulties will arise if someone is in that type of residential home, with its strongly influenced and confined atmosphere, and actually does not belong there, but still must live there and can't escape it. Then no fruitful work can occur. I didn't notice it so much the first time I went there, and that time was very happy with the children. The last few months, though, were really not easy, especially because I knew that nothing I could do would satisfy Fräulein Schulze. But I can only say that there was such tension in my life and work because of the discord, that it was impossible for me to accomplish anything and actually the only option for me was to leave. Despite everything, I have much to be grateful to Gettenbach for, as I learned a lot there and have to respect it. I hope to have been able to clarify this situation enough to you through these words so that you can understand a little why I have disappointed you so much. I don't know to what extent this is due to a lack of educational and social talent – often enough I have doubted that they even exist in me.

Everyone in Thale will certainly be looking forward to the first of Advent now, and I'm sure there are many secrets everywhere. I am sending you and all in Thale many warm greetings for the first of Advent. It will surely be a very beautiful day once again.

And now many heartfelt greetings from your

Annemarie Wächter

Anni later told:

I still stayed home for Christmas, as I could not bring myself to leave my mother before Christmas. But very soon after, I wrote to Emi-Margret that I would be coming, and I packed to go. My mother didn't know how strongly I felt about the community, but she sensed it and found my departure extremely hard. Humanly seen, I can well understand it: she was very much alone with no husband, Reinhold studying away from home, and my sister was quite sick.

7.

At the Sparhof

Sparhof, January 11, 1932

Dear Mama and Hilde,

Now I've already been here at the Sparhof for a few hours. I had good connections the whole way and good seats. Everything went smoothly and according to schedule. In Fulda I had almost two hours to wait so I went to see the cathedral and another church. The weather was really beautiful.

From Neuhof I came up by wagon and arrived at about half past four. There is still a little snow up here. Today was a very moving day. The sister of Emi-Margret's mother died this morning. She died from tuberculosis of the lungs. She had a very difficult but beautiful death.

I share my room with a little boy and four more little children sleep next door. Everything is already unpacked and put away. So you don't need to worry at all!

Many greetings to you from your

Anni

In actual fact, Anni's arrival affected her more profoundly than her letter home indicates. She later told:

When my train arrived in Neuhof, I didn't know how to get to the Sparhof, but at the station was a sleigh with horses. Arno and Trudi, who were there waiting for me, told me that only a few hours before, Emi-Margret's aunt Else von Hollander had passed away. Trudi was on her way to Fulda to get some necessary things, and I drove up to the community with Arno.

Everything was white and in deep winter, and snow covered the hills. On the way I was quite apprehensive about how it would be on the community after such a thing had happened. I imagined there would be a very heavy and sad atmosphere. But when I arrived, Emi-Margret's father greeted me with great warmth, and I immediately felt that there was no reason for my fear.

It is hard to describe the atmosphere that was in the community when I arrived. One felt something from eternity – even to me as a person who didn't especially believe in these things or look for them. There was joy in spite of the great pain of the loss.

Else von Hollander had contracted tuberculosis as a result of the poor living conditions at the Sparhof, and had been sent to Switzerland the previous year to recuperate in the mountain air, returning home in time for Emi-Margret's wedding in July. By then, it was clear that the cure had not worked. She continued her work in the community's publishing house for as long as she was able, and then, bedridden in a little hut that had been built for her, endured the ravages of her illness – a Leviathan, she called it, eating her from the inside. In dying, she experienced visions of the next world, which she recounted to those around her. "It is so wonderful that I am allowed to go into another world – the most wonderful place there is." Because of her faith and joyful anticipation of the journey she was about to begin, her death was not a morose event. Rather, it confirmed for the community members the deepest beliefs upon which their way of life was based.

In the days following Anni's arrival at the Sparhof, she heard Emi-Margret and her family describe Else's last days and her expectant certainty of the life to come. For Anni, whose Christian belief was all but extinct, these accounts had a decisive effect.

Daily life at the Sparhof was busy for Anni, who was assigned to live with and care for five of the foster children that the community had taken in.

Sparhof, January 17, 1932

My dear, good Mama and Hilde,

Now I have already been here a week. The week flew by because everything was so new to me. But I'm finding my way pretty well now. A lot has changed since I was here last. Three new houses have been built and alterations have been made in the kitchen and on the farm. Emi-Margret showed me everything yesterday.

In one house is a bakery with a big new oven where the baking is done every week. However, this is done by the men. There are around ninety people here now, and new people keep coming. Because of the death, everything was a bit different than usual and now it's gradually falling back into the usual pattern. Else von Hollander is the first one who has died here at the community. She must have been an extraordinary person. People often speak about her. The burial was also extremely solemn and festive.

I already wrote to you that I am living in the so-called children's house. It's a very nice group of children. I share a room with the five youngest, all boys. They get up at seven in the morning, and I help them dress and have breakfast with them downstairs. Then somebody else comes to look after them, and I tidy and clean the children's house. After lunch I settle them for a rest time.

We adults eat around 12:15. The noon meal often lasts a long time because something is read aloud, spoken, or we sing. After the meal I take care of the school children, about fourteen in all. When it's possible we play outside. That is very enjoyable. Afterwards I also have coffee with them.

After that I either mend or wash clothes or whatever else is needed. At about 5:45 p.m. the little ones come home to be washed. The grown-ups have supper at about 6:30. This again lasts until 7:30 or 8:00.

Everyone here received me very kindly and everyone is very friendly to me. I see Emi-Margret often, especially because we work together. She has a very nice apartment in the upper floor of the children's house.

The weather here has not been particularly inviting. For the first few days it wasn't at all bright, only a thick fog. Yesterday evening there was a wonderful sunset. The elevation here is about 1500 feet and we have a wonderful view.

I just received Mama's loving Sunday letter – thank you very much. Next time I will tell you more. For today, loving greetings from your

Anni

Sparhof, January 1932

Dear Mama and Hilde,

Time certainly flies! Already it's almost Sunday again. On Sunday January 24 there will be a double wedding. On account of the recent death, the wedding will be celebrated in a very serious way. Because of this it will be especially impressive.

Life here is rich in variety and almost every day something new happens. There are continually guests from varying backgrounds who are interested to learn about the cause we are living for.

Living together with the children is wonderful. They are very lively and very independent. If you do something special with them they are so excited and participate so enthusiastically. There are about fourteen school children, and a few older ones. There are eight kindergarten children. When the weather is somewhat nice at noon we go out. Behind the buildings is a little hill, the so-called Küppel. It is completely overgrown with juniper, heather, and other bushes. Scattered between are several beautiful big beech trees. The Küppel is a wonderful place to play. We build little huts and play hiding games. Unfortunately the last few days it has been foggy again, but the hoarfrost made everything outside look very beautiful (what we could see of it).

For us the weather is pleasant as long as everything is frozen. Otherwise everything gets terrifically dirty from the mud and slush since the yard isn't paved yet.

Everyone here is very friendly to me, especially Emi-Margret's mother, but really everyone else as well. Emi-Margret and I get along very well, so I am very happy and feel quite at home already. Three of us are working in the children's house: in addition to Emi-Margret there is also another nursery-school teacher, who is also very nice, and we work well together.

Before I forget it: please send me my official notice of departure from the mayor. I hadn't thought of this at all.

How are you all? Are you all well?

Now many loving greetings for Sunday and also a fat Sunday kiss from your

Anni

 This is the fat kiss.

Sparhof, January 25, 1932

My dear sweet Hilde-sister,

Here are many loving birthday wishes and most importantly a big fat birthday kiss. Hopefully you can have a bit of real birthday celebration together and a pleasant birthday tea. I will think of you a lot tomorrow.

Today we had a birthday celebration here with the children. One of my five boys had his seventh birthday. We celebrated with cake and cocoa. The little boy beamed all over and was very happy.

The double wedding is also over now. Both couples are on their honeymoon for a few days. A number of relatives came as guests for the occasion. On Saturday afternoon the couples went in a wagon to the registrar, and when they returned we had a festive meal. The older children were there and during the meal recited some really fine poems by Rückert. There was also a lot of singing. Responding to something that was said by the father of one of the brides, Emi-Margret's father spoke at length about the purpose of the life here, very clearly and convincingly. The celebration ended with a song sung all together. It made a deep impression on everyone. When we went outside there was a clear moonlit night with hoarfrost, so beautiful that no one wanted to go to bed, so we took a little walk on the Küppel.

The next day, Sunday, I took care of the kindergarten until noon. First there was a meeting of the inner circle of the community with the couples. At twelve o'clock was the public celebration in which all the guests took part. Emi-Margret's father led this part of the meeting, which included the actual exchange of vows. It was very solemn and festive. The couples were asked some very solemn and important questions to which they had to answer yes. For instance they were asked whether they were prepared, if one of the two would become unfaithful to the cause we live for, the other would rather give up the marriage than also become unfaithful.

Then at 3:00 there was a meal that lasted very long. Much was read and sung. Immediately after the meal the two couples departed, and we all had coffee. The weather was beautiful, real spring weather, and the tables were nicely decorated with catkins.

Just think, this was the sixth wedding at the Sparhof since last summer. Another couple is hoping to get married, but that will be later. They are actually guests that are here now and have decided to stay. They came as an engaged couple and will be married in the foreseeable future. He is an engineer from Sweden. His college gave him a scholarship to do practical work abroad for a year. When he got to know the community he decided to stay here and break off his educational trip. The school in Sweden was very generous and did not cause any difficulties, not even concerning the money.

I have to stop telling now or it will get late. Many, many greetings to both of you and to you, dear Hilde, a very big birthday kiss.

Your Anni

Say hello to the staff from me. Also many thanks for your loving Sunday letter, which made me very happy.

Sparhof, February 6, 1932

My dear Mama, Hilde, and Reinhold,

I was very happy for Mama's loving Sunday greeting. In the meantime I've also received the nice little package from Hilde. That sweet little birthday packet found favor with my five little ones. How nice that you were able to celebrate Hilde's birthday in such a happy way. And then I was also so happy for the news that Hanna visited you. That must really have been nice for you.

The days go by so quickly here that Sunday comes around again before you know it. That's also why my letters arrive at somewhat irregular intervals. It's not always so easy to plan time for writing because the unexpected often occurs – meetings, for instance. It is wonderful that I can spend so much time with Emi-Margret, much better even than in Thale, because here one is able to be much more free and at home than there.

I don't know how much of the community and its life you can already imagine. I would really like you to become well acquainted with the character of the way of life here. Up until now I have actually told you more about the outward aspects and less about the actual aims. When one is here many things appear so self-evident that it doesn't even occur to one to write about them. But today I wanted to write you a bit about the meaning of the communal work, as far as I have understood it up to now.

The first and foremost thing is this, that people have gathered together here in order to live their lives filled by a clearly defined and common purpose. It is a community of people from the most varied classes and professions who have come out of groups with the most diverse world outlooks, for instance the Religious Socialists, the Socialist Party, the Youth Movement, and religious circles of all kinds, etc. They wish to live and work–and also even be ready to die–for one common goal. They are affiliated neither with a mainstream church nor a political party, and also obey the government only insofar as its demands do not conflict with their convictions. The one and only thing to which they feel themselves bound is contained in the words of the Bible, especially the New Testament. That means, they feel deeply gripped by and committed to what comes to us through the Bible from God, the coming of his kingdom, the sending out of his Holy Spirit, the life of Jesus, and what he requires of mankind. This compelled them to such a degree that they had to break off their former lives that they had been leading within the framework of the normal middle-class world, in order to place their entire lives and whole strength from then on into the service of discipleship to Christ and in the faith and hope in the kingdom of God.

The fundamental thing–always hard to grasp at first–is that through an encounter with the divine they received such a great faith that they were able to discard all obstacles from their former lives in order to dedicate their whole lives until death to the new task and direction which they recognized because of their faith in God. This will be especially difficult to understand in our time in which there are so few people willing to live and die in a manner consistent with their convictions. The community members believe in God and his Trinity as an absolute reality. He is the first and the last Truth. He is reality; there is none greater. To them, he is neither a beautiful ideal arising from the affectations of the emotional life nor an indeterminate, problematic entity.

I felt just how real this faith is, how completely free of falsity, when I heard about the death of Else von Hollander. She truly received powers from another world through her sacrificing faith: it would not have been possible for her to overcome her excruciatingly painful physical death so victoriously in any other way. Death was no longer anything heavy, dark, or oppressive. Rather, it was simply the entrance to the inconceivable kingdom of eternity, and freedom from the earthly. This death has become a powerful testimony to the truth of an unshakeable, childlike, surrendered faith. Such an experience of faith is, of course, initially the purely personal experience of each individual. But the nature of God that is revealed to people through such an experience confronts them with the call to life in community.

God is love, faithfulness, grace, mercy, and justice. God loves all people as his children and no one is greater than another. That is why all people should love each other as brothers. It is not possible to create a life of love and brotherliness within the fragmentation of the existing social order. The communal way of life alone can foster such relationships. That has absolutely nothing to do with the sweetly pacifistic attitude that calls every man a brother. It is not always easy to recognize the brother in every man, and not to believe oneself higher and better than another. That holds true not only in personal relationships but also in the attitudes of whole groups of people, even of whole countries, towards each other. Such a stance necessarily leads to conscientious objection to war and to the bearing of arms, because a consistent adherence to a life of love will not tolerate violence in any form.

Living by love implies a life of social justice, because love encompasses each person equally–it cannot show partiality. Therefore the type of communal life that is lived here cannot recognize the generally established class distinctions. There are no higher or lower social classes for the members here. A person's family name does not make him a better person. And economic injustice can be accepted just as little as human injustice. Such a community must reject capitalism and desire to live in complete community of goods, in the communism of the original apostolic church. Personal property and earnings are completely renounced.

You will understand now why there can be no payment of wages for work done here. All egoistic impulses, all selfishness and self-will must be combated. As soon as we begin to look out for our own interests, loving service towards others ceases. Only when we free ourselves from everything that binds us to property and possessions can we be given a life of love; only then are we able to follow Christ. This community has therefore taken a life of simplicity and poverty voluntarily upon itself. Because it is only through this voluntary poverty that a life of social justice, one that is increasingly free from material and temporal things, can be found. Such a life points to irrevocable and final values, to the eternal. Put into practice, it means that in this community of currently around ninety people there is no private enterprise through which each individual would seek to acquire as much as he could for himself. Whatever a person owns they give to the community. Whatever support and necessities he or she needs is provided by the community.

Such a life in community therefore means a battle against the egoistic nature of humankind. It cannot be carried out in comfort and self-satisfied tranquility. Every uncompromising stance requires struggle, effort, and loyalty. In just the same way this life calls for concentration, privation, hardship, sacrifice, martyrdom. The people here know that they want to–and must–go this way just as Christ had to endure death on the cross in order to rise again. By doing this he did not relieve us from having to go the same way, but rather showed it to us by example. And because all here are conscious of the difficulty and bitterness of the way, there is no sweetly gushing Christianity, no false enthusiasm that fades into thin air with empty phrases (as one may be tempted to think), but rather a Christianity of true conviction and faith and therefore a Christianity of deeds. That is the pivotal thing. As part of its ultimate goal and through the strength of God and his spirit, this Christianity seeks to penetrate the whole of life right down into the smallest practical details. It undertakes this with ardent zeal and exertion. It is precisely in the most mundane routines of daily life–those that are not filled by the elation of holier hours–that this Christianity must be tested lest it remain empty and useless. Then everyone will see that the great cause must be made alive and visible through deeds, through actions.

And by that I mean the right kind of deeds. Personal emotionalism and personal wishes could never be allowed to sully the character of the great cause, rendering it feeble and artificial. No, the great cause requires an objective course of action in all things. And the wonderful thing is the extent to which the community lives out this cause in actual deeds. Firstly, how every realization of the truth is translated into deed. That means that everything opposed to the nature of the cause is rejected in reality (private life in the ordinary sense, egoism, wealth, violence, etc. are renounced) and everything that fosters the nature of the cause finds its birth in reality (life in community, an open door, loyalty and purity, etc.). And secondly, all daily practical work can only be done well if it is done in the spirit of the cause. And therefore a lot of work is also really accomplished. That is the difference to all the many intentional communities that have, as you know, almost all failed: here everything is done under the clear sign of the one great goal. All work therefore simply has to be done, and does get done quite naturally and objectively.

Such objectivity means clarity, purity, truth. It cannot tolerate any half-heartedness or compromise, only a clear all or nothing. The greatness of the cause demands a pure, responsible decision from all those who want to live here to serve in true faithfulness, poverty, and willingness. A person must wish to joyfully and completely surrender their own will and strive to overcome all egoism. This way demands the joyful, voluntary shouldering of all bitterness and hardships of this way. It demands a constant focusing of all capacities in order not to lose sight of the goal.

And yet this all remains senseless human efforts and decisions unless one is given the conviction that it cannot be otherwise; that one can and must act. The life of the community is not something that can be lived by a decision of the will or the intellect. Heart and soul—one's entire being—must be gripped by this cause. Once the reality of, and the coming of God's kingdom—for this is the name of the cause—is revealed in even the tiniest corner of a person, it causes them to radically change the direction of their life in order to become ever more open and receptive to this reality of the kingdom of God. The task is so great that each person must find a wholly child-like heart in order to serve the cause in the deepest sense, in full trust, true humility, and surrender, and be overwhelmed ever anew by its greatness.

The Sparhof community thus has a difficult, but great task in front of it—one that must demand of people every effort and the dedication of every strength. Clearly then, living here cannot be an arbitrary stay for as long as it suits a person, a temporary refuge for times in which one doesn't know where else to go. That would be a misinterpretation of the open door, which demands a clear decision in each case, either for or against.

I have decided for the life of this community. That means that my life and work from now on belong to this cause. You must not think that my decision was influenced by my friendship with Emi-Margret. It is of course wonderful to be able to live with her here, but ultimately that is not the determining factor because–as I have pointed out–our lives do not belong to us personally but rather to the cause.

It is certainly true that the people here have completely committed themselves and that I too have now completely committed myself. But the goal is so great that one readily gives up one's personal freedom and the possibility of exploring the world at will for the privilege of living for the cause. I can't imagine any future work that would be greater and more worthwhile than that here. I only hope that through this letter you are able to understand a little of how I came to this decision, and that it is impossible for me to return to the former way of life. As strange and incomprehensible as this may seem to you, I still hope very much that you may be able to understand this step. Actually it is nothing that could separate us personally.

I am very happy with my resolution. I have been a novice for about a week. This is a longer trial period of about a year, possibly longer, that precedes admittance into the membership circle. But now I have already written a great deal so goodbye, and many many greet-ings from your

Anni

D I A R Y

February 21, 1932

What has happened during this time?

In regard to me, a lot. It is all so tremendous and unfathomable. How to comprehend that the living God has come into life—into my life? We venture to ask him that we might be allowed to encounter him and thereby live a life of dedication and love after the example of his son Jesus Christ. Who could ever have anticipated such a reality? And yet, for me it is not the certainty of a child.

8.

A Fixed Point

Anni's letter was received in Keilhau with considerable shock. It was hardly a month since she had gone to the Sparhof, and now she was writing to inform her family that she had made a lifetime vow of loyalty to a group of whose aims and beliefs they were ignorant.

The effects of Anni's decision were profound. As a novice member, she had committed herself to a life of voluntary poverty and renounced her career and personal plans. Living conditions at the Sparhof were poor, and the work was demanding. Anni had also assumed the community's religious dress—long skirts and a head kerchief. Frau Wächter wrote to her daughter begging for further explanation of this step and enumerating the many objections that arose in her mind.

Sparhof, February 28, 1932

Dear Mama, Hilde, and Reinhold,

Thank you very much for Mama's loving answer and

the lovely little spring package. Where did those two snowdrops come from? Everyone who sees them is amazed. I got them both last Saturday/Sunday. But now I first want to answer you about Mama's letter.

I would gladly have told you something of the nature of life here earlier, but at that time I realized things more in isolated parts and not in the all-encompassing great-ness of the cause. And the cause always continues to grow the more it is revealed to an individual – even if only tiny parts are disclosed at a time.

I don't think the attitude of the people here towards the task they have been given came through clearly enough in my last letter.

The community has heard from many sides the accu-sation that it is easy to pull back from the world with its social, political, cultural, and class-based structure, to denounce these and live like hermits, sheltered, undis-turbed, and apart. And the individual is told that it is easier to accomplish something under the protection and security of the community than to blaze his or her path alone. I think that neither the one nor the other is actu-ally as simple and easy as such words might make it seem.

Don't you think that a cause that prompts people to make a completely radical and uncompromising break with all the unscrupulousness, untruthfulness, and injus-tice which they, as so many others, had previously made such comfortable use of in social, business, and personal life – don't you think that such a cause must really have something to it if people are ready to dedicate themselves to it so unreservedly?

Because, by disassociating themselves from their former ways of life, people also break with the comforts and conveniences associated with that life and take upon themselves everything that such a different way of living brings with it, such as misunderstandings, ridicule, mockery, hostilities, and malicious gossip. They take all difficulties of the new way of life upon themselves.

Very often when people are moved by some spiritual power to a radical renunciation of previously existing conditions – as it happened in the revolution or the Youth Movement, for example – they return again to the world of concessions and double standards after only once taking a principled position or action. So then perhaps it is not quite as easy to dismiss a community that has sought to preserve its radical – that is, clear, distinct, and unadulterated – position for twelve years so far; a community that, instead of blurring the lines of its convictions, continually sought and seeks to clarify and purify them yet more.

And as it happens, the isolation from the world and its happenings is only external. Inwardly, a very strong interest in and solidarity towards world events prevails. This of course provokes a very definite response to various incidents. This life in community is not to be compared to an order of monks who eliminate all worldly pleasures in their striving towards personal blessedness and union with God. Rather, it means seeking with all people who look for a meaning in life, and finding unity and community in the belief in the kingdom of God and the power of his Spirit. This is what it is, not each small person's plea and demand for their own salvation. No, it is the certainty that all who are ready will be equally blessed by the Spirit–there is no stairway to salvation on which a person can climb to a certain height of blessedness according to their own merit and worthiness.

The gift of God and the gift of the Holy Spirit is a gift that is available for all who are open to it. And therefore the isolation of the community here is actually an illusion. We cannot know to what extent others who don't live in outward community with those here have opened their hearts to all this, and how much has been revealed to them unbeknownst to us. It is not true that this community is trying to gain a monopoly on a deeper interpretation of life through some sort of proud collective egoism that completely rejects all other types of people and lifestyles. Rather, they wish to reach out from their attempt at a clear and uncompromising way of life to find all those who feel the same longing but who have their tasks to fulfill in other places. In all humility and disregard for their own personal deeds and decisions, they wish to advocate for the fulfillment of a common goal. The message that the people here have received should therefore be carried more actively than ever to all other people, so that all who feel the same longing may become completely aware of this calling. Nobody here thinks that this community is the only possible community or that it portrays the only possible way of acting and doing. And the coming of that for which we all hope–namely the kingdom of God and his justice–is not dependent on the work and life of the Sparhof community in the form in which it exists here, but rather, it depends on the willingness and dedication of all those who know themselves to be a part of this direction and purpose.

I don't know if I already told you that there are communities in America whose whole direction and purpose is completely aligned with ours. They have already existed for over 400 years and are called the Hutterite Brothers. They currently have about 3000 members. The community here has joined them. The inner life of their communities is still as pure, living, and original as it was at the time of their formation. By the mere fact of their long history, these Hutterite communities are evidence of the truth and reality of what the community here also seeks and wishes for.

Now I'll come to your other point, namely the objection that it must be much easier to achieve things within a community than to do them on one's own. I don't think at all that it is so much easier. In the first place, I don't believe that it's so easy and simple for people to attune themselves completely to the purpose and direction of the community: to give up all ambitions that lead to personal possessions and advantage, not only outwardly but from within; to act neither mentally nor physically out of private interest; to live not in self-will but with the communal good in mind. Do you really believe that a community of around eighty people can live in peace and joy with one another in complete community of goods, without unpeace or spitefulness–just like that, without any further ado?

And then of course, in the deepest sense, to put oneself at the disposal of the communal life does not mean – as I already wrote at one point – finding a security and safety that relieves an individual of any personal responsibility. Living in community doesn't mean escaping from the struggle for existence that is directly based on a person's income and expenses. From the economic perspective, the community also depends on each member's efforts to secure its continuance. And so the need to provide for oneself is only seemingly lifted from each individual.

But living in community also does not mean release from the responsibility of personal decisions where questions of the inner path are concerned. By giving up self-will and independence, one is not categorically giving up personal responsibility towards any wish, any action, or any decision – in other words towards any deed of any kind – because the community will take care of it in one's stead; no, all of these are merely given a new direction. One person, as an individual, can only represent his or her perception of life, of work, of the government, etc. and his or her accomplishments toward that end – provided the individual is guided by the urgings of an inner voice to which he or she listens – are on an equally small scale. But now the individual steps out of the boundaries of his own circle of influence and becomes part of the wide, sweeping circle of the community.

In the community, however, the individual cannot go his own way for himself, rather, all are gripped by one spirit and each represents the whole. And it becomes each one's personal responsibility to be conscious of the measure to which they seek to serve the whole, to what extent they belong to it, and that they continue to feel ever more strongly drawn to and committed to it.

The individual in the community is responsible to see that no idol of personal ideals arises in him to cloud the clarity of the cause. He carries this responsibility on the one hand as an individual towards his community and on the other as a representative of his community towards the rest of the world. A weakening of clarity in thought or belief must not be allowed on any side, unless the essence of the whole is to be risked. I think that that is a very great responsibility, and I think it must be at least as great as that which is taken on by someone who (insofar as they accept any responsibility at all) lives in the middle of public life, swaying back and forth between the constantly changing influences of every prevailing wind, never able to completely embrace either one way or the other, and trying to find – at best – an acceptable middle ground.

I truly hope that I've been able to explain to you, at least in some measure, that life in the community here is not to be compared to a monastic hermit life in which one happily lets the world and its inhabitants go for the sake of following one's most personal inner longings in inviolate isolation. The events of current public life must be followed and considered with lively interest and should serve to lead the community to a clear stance and course of action. This view of things may be somewhat foreign to you since it is taken from a different watch-tower than the one from which you look out upon the world. But it's important to stress that there is no desire to hide our life and seeking here behind convent walls, to live in peace and seclusion. No, we wish to be bold in speaking clearly, openly, and publicly about this inner-most conviction—that means, to lay our beliefs out to anyone who wishes to hear them and to substantiate them through deeds.

Now you will certainly ask me why I of all people want to live in community; why don't I want to live as an individual as I have up to now, or find new tasks and goals—and why does it necessarily have to be this community?

There's not really that much more I can say in answer. There simply can be no other goal for me after what I was allowed to experience here, as much as you may want to consider me an impulsive convert, someone who has suddenly gone pious, eccentric, or maybe completely insane. There is no lack of possible work and tasks in this world, but I've already tried throughout this whole letter to demonstrate to you just why it has to be community in exactly the form in which it's understood here. An isolated individual can never achieve his goal. Once he completely recognizes the demands and scope of his goal, he will find that he must step out of isolation and reach toward others in brotherly gesture—and then commu-nity is formed. If he believes, however, that he is able to persist in his isolation, the deepest truth and purpose behind everything have not yet been revealed to him.

I think that you will now realize that there can be no other way for me, despite your objections. And that I stand firmly by everything I wrote you in my previous letter. You can believe me when I say that. I don't wish to hurt you with this, but it must be as it is. It would only be sad for me to think you might imagine that through this step I am breaking off my relationship to you. That is not even possible. We belong to each other in spite of everything, even if many miles separate us, because we are still bound to each other by bonds deeper than our worldviews or political or vocational connections. And it's not possible for the picture that I carry within me of you, of our life together, and of our home to be disturbed or destroyed by this new step. If you could only please understand that. But I have to refuse your offer to come home for Easter. Nonetheless, I am very sorry to have to leave the whole Fröbel work to Reinhold. But there really wouldn't be any point in it because we would just torture ourselves and maybe still be too much at cross-purposes. Because you have to believe me that you will not be able to dissuade me from this way. But please do write your objections to me so that I can try to answer you as best as I'm able. I would be glad if Reinhold could write once. Maybe I can visit you at a later date. It would also be nice if one of you could visit me here sometime, so that you can form your own impressions of this life. (Of course, it doesn't have to be immediately.)

Many thanks for all of your news – I am interested

in it all. I was especially glad that Reinhold was able to submit his doctoral thesis. I'll write you soon about what all is happening here.

But for now many greetings.

Love from your Anni

I am very happy and doing very well.

Sparhof, March 6, 1932

Dear Mama, Hilde, and Reinhold,

This last week has been quite spring-like, so that we were able to be outside with the children quite often. Earlier it was bitterly cold with a very strong east wind blowing and the temperature sinking to −32°C at night. Hopefully now it won't get so cold anymore. We're hoping there will soon be some snowdrops–there are a lot growing wild in the woods around here. You don't need to be worried that I might have suffered from the cold. On account of the children, our two rooms are heated every evening, and every morning too during the worst of the cold. And of course we hardly use those rooms during the day. Lighting the stove was difficult for me at first, but now I'm quite adept at it.

Emi-Margret's father is traveling–he's doing preliminary work in various cities for talks that some from here will give about what the community stands for and our way of life. They used to do this often in earlier years but had stepped back from it somewhat lately because the inner building up of the community demanded all their strength and time. Emi-Margret's mother has now started to write down the story of the beginning of the community in Sannerz near Schlüchtern, and the initial stages of communal life. It is then read aloud after dinner and makes the growth of the community so alive for us. It sprang from such an amazing life and movement and had to weather so many storms and difficulties of both an inner and outer nature that it's really a miracle that the cause prevailed and can be built up today. There are also plenty of humorous incidents and we often have to laugh out loud.

My work and life with the children is wonderful. From next week on I won't be directly with the children anymore because then Emi-Margret will start working with the babies and I will take over her work. Then I will either have the kindergarten in the mornings or the youngest school children from 10:00 o'clock on for arts and crafts. I will be with the school children in the midday, until 3:00 o'clock, and then in the afternoons I'll supervise the elementary school children's play and keep them occupied, or I'll have the kindergarten. And in the evenings I'll put the kindergarten children to bed.

Middays with the children have always been especially fun. I often went with the children to the so-called "black brook" which edges on a little copse. The children love to build very sweet little huts there. Then they are always enthusiastic and completely absorbed. I sometimes bring a book with me and sit in the sun. One can let the children play quite freely. They only occasionally come running up to me to ask something.

I have agreed with Emi-Margret that I'll take the school children, especially the five fourth-graders, on longer hikes as soon as it gets warmer. First we'll go for one day and then also for several days into the Rhön hills, to Dammersfeld, the Kreuzberg, etc. We are all looking forward to that very much. Hopefully we can begin soon.

I think of you all very often. And greet you very, very much and send you all a little kiss.

Your Anni

If Mama hasn't started my sweater yet please send me the yarn – the long mealtimes and also often the meetings present a good opportunity to work on something like that; the others also do. We do a lot of knitting here and I could knit or crochet the sweater.

Sparhof, March 13, 1932

My dear Mama, Hilde, and Reinhold,

Thank you very much for all of your letters; I especially enjoyed the little bunch of violets from Hilde. It arrived totally fresh, and now it's still standing on my table. It won't be easy for me to answer your letters, but I have to tell you as strongly as I can that I think of you all with great love.

But I must tell you right from the beginning that I have to answer no to all your requests and entreaties. I find it very difficult, and it seems almost impossible to me to make you understand this no. And yet I want to explain to you, as strongly as I possibly can, that there really can be nothing else for me, no other decision, but that this is the decision. If this decision would not stand now, all that I wrote you in my previous letters, far from representing a decision, would be meaningless prattle, artificial sympathies, a reveling in sentimentality. But this decision – which troubles you so much, that I can understand so well – is not an irresponsible and unscrupulous abandonment of the duties I would have had in Keilhau. It is not a desertion, because it was not in my power to either stay or flee; this decision is not influenced by any person nor any group of people; neither was it made by any willful resolution of mine. It was not made or engineered by any human being, rather, I was simply gripped by it. The only thing that I could do in response was to let myself be seized by this decision as fully as possible. But actually even this did not lie in my power alone.

You must not think that I don't understand or don't want to grasp just how great the plight is in which you now find yourselves, and that the situation has especially come to a head now. I can imagine it all so vividly, even though I also would very much like to have a complete and exact description of the facts and events and plead with you to write me everything in detail. But I will not be able to help you in the way in which you would wish. That path is not mine; I have been shown another one from which there is no turning back. Although it may seem very harsh to you, I still have to tell you that nothing will or should be able to bind me more deeply and strongly than that which has become clear to me upon this path. Nobody, not even one's closest relatives, can dissuade or persuade another in this matter. It is something that must happen quite personally within an individual, be they twenty or forty years old. Something is truly separated and resolved within a person in the sense of purification and cleansing.

I could not have foreseen any more than you that I would make this decision so soon. It also could not have been discussed or deliberated – I was simply gripped by a different power in such a way that I had to leave everything else behind me, even what seemed to be the most strongly binding human obligations. And I had to do it – and was able to do it – even in full knowledge of what this step would mean for you. You won't believe that of me. And yet it is true that I was conscious of the consequences and impact of this step, and that my objective reasoning was not shoved aside by a wave of mystical feeling. So this decision cannot be explained away as the consequence of ecstatic excitement, to be abandoned in favor of the former conventional way of life once all is examined under the sober light of day.

You must also not imagine that I was pressed or compelled to take this step by the people here, or that my actions occurred more or less under the power of suggestion. They would certainly have gladly let me go without trying to hold me back if my decision had been otherwise. In fact, it would not have been right in such a case for me to wish to stay on longer here because this life is not meant to be a mere mutual aid co-operative. What urged me to this step and decision was something that I was able to experience quite personally, and it determined this way for me quite personally. It really was an encounter with another world.

It's not easy for me to write about what I can barely express with words. But I wanted to attempt it in order to show you as clearly as possible how compelling all of this has become for me, and also that neither appeals to youthful immaturity, nor criticism of my reasoning, nor human obligations and ties can reverse this decision. It has nothing to do with my personal happiness, with my inner peace in the fulfillment of my aims and wishes, or with the well-being of my soul. It is, therefore, not a matter of what is easier or more difficult for me; my sole concern is to do only what is in keeping with this decision. I was never under the illusion that I had chosen the more difficult way—I don't think I could have been so arrogant as to believe that. I only believe that I must completely and wholeheartedly do what this new way demands of me and of everyone else to whom it has been revealed.

And now you will again ask why I can't do this in Keilhau among you there. And why I can't put my "Christianity of deeds and the gospel of love" into practice there? I must reply that it is not just a matter of simply doing, loving, and helping, as I had formerly imagined it to be. Rather, it is a matter of an active Christianity of love and service in the name of Christ that can only occur in the sense of a renewal and rebirth of the old man. That means it cannot occur where there is discord, where it is considered acceptable to apply violence against violence and hate against hate. It cannot occur in a socially unjust and callous surrounding. Such a life must be lived in the place where there is a wish for unanimity and a readiness for unity that desires and prays for true surrender in loving service. It must be a place where the anticipation and promise of the kingdom of God translates into living deeds, and where unity results from this one Spirit.

I cannot write more about this now. I would like to respond to Reinhold's letter separately at some point. For now, I'll just write that he is warmly invited to come here sometime for a few days, so that he may discuss his various questions with us in person. Everyone here would welcome such a debate.

I think of you all very often and wish so much that you would be able to understand it all, as incomprehensible as it may still seem.

Greeting you with all my love,

your Anni

D I A R Y

Easter Sunday, March 25, 1932

One thinks it has been overcome and the matter is quite clear. Then you need only read between the lines of the letters, and it is all opened up again. They don't need to write a single word about it, but there is so much grief and sadness and pain between the lines that I can hardly get over it. A feeling of guilt comes over me again and again. Can I really do it? I have asked myself so many times already. By my actions I am destroying the lives of two people, and in Reinhold's case it is somehow the core of his life. But my leaving will cause Mama and Hilde a rent in their inmost being, a rent which they will never overcome. There is no doubt that my leaving would shorten their lives. I am taking away their joy and confidence in life so that I can live a life of joyful dedication. Do I really have a right to do that? Is that God's will? It is so difficult.

D I A R Y

April 6, 1932

I think it will simply have to come to a very painful and bitter parting of our ways, as Reinhold indicated. I don't want to think about it—it will be so hard and painful. I would not have thought the separation would be so hard. One does not like to speak about it, for how insignificant is this struggle in view of the greatness and the victory of the whole cause. But for me personally there will have to be a clear decision, otherwise I will constantly feel incomplete. I don't know how I will find my way through. It is so infinitely hard. Sometimes I almost wish I had never experienced this, and then I wouldn't have to feel so divided. The worst part of it is not the separation from those at home as I personally feel it, which is constantly getting more severe and deep and painful. How glad I would be to bear that alone, however much it hurts. The worst part is knowing how badly I am hurting my family, what great need I am leaving them in, and how I am only causing greater and greater need. It is through me and my fault that their joy and confidence and courage for life are being completely extinguished, physically as well as inwardly.

I see it all so clearly before me. Is such a thing possible? I don't understand it, I can't understand it. There simply must be a solution. Is it really meant to be that way? I can't grasp it. Then Christ is very far away from me. Where does this great love and affection between parents and children come from, that one can and may trample on it like that? I don't know where to turn. The only times I speak about it, I do so in a rather ironic, light tone, and it feels each time as if I am betraying them and disowning them.

And yet there has to be a clear way. Isn't the love between parents and children something that is willed and given by God? How can one destroy it? And yet I have to do this. I ask myself over and over again, have I really allowed myself to be gripped by the important thing here? Am I following it truly, and not just literally? It sometimes seems to me as if in my inner life I am just as lifeless and unmoved as before. I don't know what to do. I realize more and more how much my inner and outward actions are lacking in true life and the real fire of love, so that I cannot grasp anything, and nothing grips me.

As long as this is so, I do not have the clarity and conviction to write to them. I ask fervently for clarity. It can't go on like this. Something has to happen.

And then on the other hand it is a fact that I am

sure – really inwardly, not with my mind – that I cannot
let go of this life. Hard as it often is simply to believe, it
is infinitely reassuring and strengthening to know that
there is an absolute truth, an infinitely great love, and
that everything does not melt away in indefinite relativism. And it is just as wonderful to know that one does
not have to squander and waste one's life, one does not
need to ask anymore what life is actually for, what its
purpose is.

Despite an eight year difference in age, Anni and Rein-
hold were close, having grown up with the expectation
that their shared life's work would be the Keilhau school.
Reinhold, who was still following the academic course
that had also been planned for Anni, found her decision
especially bewildering.

Sparhof, April 27, 1932

Dear Reinhold,

Warm thanks for your letter of March 28. I also thank
Hilde very much for the last loving letter she wrote. And
now I've heard about your splendid results on the Latin
exam – my heartiest congratulations at this success.

The essence of life here, to which I feel committed,
is an awareness of the kingdom of God – and not just a
kingdom existing far away in some vague fantasy land
that will come at some undetermined point in time,
but a kingdom that must be lived and realized here and

now. It is not an ideology or a product of philosophical recognition and theoretical deliberation, and therefore is not dependent on the relativity of human research and thought. No, it can exist only in the living reality of deeds – in the visible result of all that we do. Only so does this kingdom correspond with the will of God. Because God himself is absolute reality. He is not created by some philosophical system, nor can he be measured by human reasoning or critical analysis. Therefore he is also no mere concept but exists – in truth – as the one who is the creator and author of all things. He encompasses all that is; from his hand springs the past, present, and future. And one can only believe in him as one believes in an absolute reality. The god we have chosen as the highest ideal recognizable by our understanding is certainly not the true God, because God cannot be grasped by our intellect – or if so, we would be capable of forming only a very human, even if perhaps well intended, picture of a godly being. This picture would be very fragmentary and contradictory, and would make God accessible only to intellectuals, to those with highly trained minds, whereas God often lives most purely in those who are simple and childlike.

Now that is not to say that there should only be simple people or, to put it bluntly, that stupidity is godly and desirable. But it does mean that we should under-stand where the limits of human reason lie and that there is much above and beyond these limits that can only be grasped by faith. And that becomes possible for the man who lets all that is human within him become silent in order to stand before the divine in adoration, reverence, and awe.

But I know that all of you – and of course we here as well – are primarily concerned with the practical mani-festation of the kingdom of God in the sense in which I have just described it. This goal is perfectly clear to me, and the Sparhof here in the Rhön hills is certainly not the only place that attempts to live for it. But not every way leads to this goal: there are very many so-called Christian ways of life that are completely and deeply opposed to it.

We wish to live in unity, social justice, brotherly surrender, and love. Unity is created through the power of the Holy Spirit: since God only reveals himself to people through the Holy Spirit's working within us, we can only find a living, direct relationship to God in this way. However, this Spirit will, and must, bring about a very strong unity and unanimity – a profound commu-nity – amongst the people who have opened themselves to it. Life in community, therefore, is not something that is initiated and constructed by people, something that they can consequently just as readily abandon. People sought unity with God, and through it unity with one another was given to them.

It would not be possible to build a community on human strengths and capabilities, as the countless unsuc-cessful intentional communities have shown. Life in community and unity is a gift of God to those who have made themselves ready to receive the working of his Holy Spirit. At the same time, it is also the will of God and his call to us because only in this way can we live in unity with him and so live for his kingdom. All strength for such a life is given us only through the unity found in community.

Everything I wrote you about the meaning and nature of the community will not, of course, be that important to you and probably won't even seem believable. But it is indeed true, and those who live in this community have continued to see proof of it throughout the past twelve years. I only thought it might be important to you as an explanation of my insistence on communal life. It also cannot be a life in just any community, in the community of family at home for example. It can only be a life in a community brought about by the power of the Holy Spirit in the sense of working and living for the kingdom of God. Such a life challenges us to live for social justice, that means, in brotherly communism, in full community. Practically seen, this means a surrender of all personal possessions to the community, a complete personal poverty. We cannot achieve any social justice by giving perhaps a small part of our property to be used for the poor, yet keeping the greater share for ourselves. This is why we are told repeatedly, "Sell everything you have and follow me." These words become especially meaningful in light of the massive unemployment and spiritual and physical suffering of so many today.

And it would not be possible for me to go back to a life of personal property and personal rights to property – I would feel a great guilt. I don't mean to say that you are living in great wealth; I know better than that. Yet it remains personal property, and after all, the whole family conflict is a quarrel over property and rights. Though I know well that the dispute over these things is not your ultimate purpose in life, nevertheless it remains a dispute, and I cannot join in. This has nothing to do with a narrow-minded or self-righteous attitude. It doesn't mean that I feel better than you or set myself above you. I simply can no longer have a part in it.

That is why I ask you to dissolve my savings account. I don't know how much it is anymore. I think you might well use it to pay the lawyer or for Hilde's medical bills (which I would much prefer) or something of this kind. Mama should transfer the money to her account. If you don't want it, please transfer it here so that it can be used for the community. Either way, please close my savings account. I don't want to have any such savings to fall back on.

So you see, freedom from all property is an essential part of community life, of living in deep inner fellowship and love. By no means do I count you among those who are indifferent to social need, but I do not find your way sufficient for a life of absolute social justice.

Now I come to what you call senseless egalitarianism. But what do achievement and reward really mean? How can achievement really be measured along with its corresponding reward? These are based on entirely human criteria. Who is to judge how much more one person has achieved than another? And where the greatest achievements lie and where again greater performance can still be expected? These are all purely subjective, human insights that change with every passing era. The real truth is that by nature we have been endowed with various gifts, which we should strive to put to use. These gifts should, however, be used in service to others, as far as is at all possible. They must be allowed to unfold to the greatest possible extent in a testimony of honor and obedience towards him from whom we have received them. But the power to judge the extent to which we have used or misused our gifts does not lie with us. Therefore we would be mistaken in wishing to demand greater rewards for ourselves based on our own insights. And isn't it true that all people have the same right to life? Who would dare to deny another person the right to life in the sense of that person's physical existence? And, what is more, who would dare to deny them the right to seek the light of truth and then live for it? Who can claim that there is no spark of longing for God, the light, in every person, however hidden it may be?

In this sense, we are all the same before God. How can we know the extent to which any one of us has followed what God laid within us? For judgment comes from God's hand alone. We can speak of the diversity of humankind only in terms of the varying gifts and talents with which each has been equipped, not only purely in character but also in regard to each one's differing capabilities. That is a fact, but certainly no judgment. Why does no one wish to recognize our equality in this sense? Why do we each wish to preserve our own egotistic individualism?

Life in community cannot be separated from an awareness of the kingdom of God. This does indeed depend on a community's particular direction and form. A life of unconditional love, for example, is not possible where violence in any form is also acceptable, even if only as a means to an end. Love can only be born of love; it can never be born of violence. It's not for nothing that we are told to "love your enemies." But it is not possible to live in this awareness of the kingdom of God unless we really feel called to it. I have to say that again and again, because what counts are the deeds that actually follow such a recognition. To talk about love, community, dedication, justice, and other ideals while living the opposite is indeed empty talk.

What I have written may seem irresponsible, hard, and cold toward you. You put the demands made on me here on the same level with those made in Keilhau, and because those came first, you feel I should give up these. I have to simply say quite bluntly that there is nothing I hold dearer than the calling of the kingdom of God – not the concept of fatherland, not the concept of home, not the concept of family ties, not the concept of free will as a purely subjective, human freedom.

I truly wish to – and must – leave behind everything which hinders that calling. We read that unless we are willing to leave father and mother, wife and children, house and home, we are not ready for discipleship. This passage has made an extremely strong impression on me ever since I arrived here. That may even mean you, if you will not understand and if you continue to see it as a betrayal on my part. But I hold on to the hope that we will reach a mutual understanding.

These words may convey only hardheartedness, forgetting, despising, and trampling underfoot of mother love and the love between brother and sister. I must tell you once more that I have not forgotten, much less despised, anything; on the contrary, it is alive in my heart, and it would be more painful than I can say if this should lead to a break. Yet if you and the family should think that no further relationship can continue between us after all that has been said, I would willingly accept such a break, even though it would hurt me deeply. Don't imagine that these things have all been plain to me from the beginning; however, it is becoming more and more clear to me that there is no other way.

Now I want to go into what you call unconditional determinism. To be gripped by God's will has nothing to do with transcendental ecstasy or vague feelings of rapture. On the contrary, this is a question of the determination of a person's will. Nor does it have anything in common with fatalism. It is true that the power of the Holy Spirit active in the community can grip and confront even a person who previously had no knowledge of it. In this way God's will and nature are also revealed to such a person—an experience so real and powerful that it leads to a completely unshakeable faith. However, it must be preceded by a certain expectant readiness for something from above. If a person lets his own petty human will rule him as an absolute god, he will obstruct the possibility of receiving this grace. But once a person has understood something of the nature and will of God, his human will begins to bend itself with all its might toward serving and glorifying the One he now knows and recognizes. He now expends his human will entirely toward living for the kingdom of God, because such knowledge can only become deed if all powers and energies of the will are exerted. Admittedly all strength of will must be received from the great, almighty will of God: a private, autonomous decision of the human will can accomplish nothing.

But now this letter is long enough.

Warmest greetings,

your sister Anni

Sparhof, April 28, 1932

My dear Mama and Hilde,

Warmest thanks for your dear letter from last Sunday. I enjoyed it very much.

Since last week spring has definitely come to our area too. We now have dry and quite warm weather. There are so many flowers blooming now. Last Monday afternoon I hiked to the Sinn River at Oberzell with the younger school children. The whole way there we walked through lovely meadows along a brook. The meadows were filled with pale yellow cowslips. Everything looked beautiful again, and we all brought big bunches of flowers home with us. Altogether it was a wonderful afternoon. We had all kinds of little experiences together, and all of our legs were very tired that evening. On Sunday afternoon I was in a beech grove where little blue periwinkles bloomed everywhere. The children love to look for flowers.

The work on the farm and garden is very urgent now

and all work strength is directed there, with everyone working very hard at it.

Our work in the kindergarten and Hort has now become much easier: we spend almost all day playing outside in some nice sunny spot. The older children mostly disappear into all possible varieties of huts, shacks, and caves which they have built themselves. The boys work hard in the fields, picking stones and pulling up quack grass. This of course isn't always pure delight for them but it has to be done.

But now I greet you most dearly and send a kiss from
your Anni

Hopefully now Hilde won't feel so cold anymore. I'm glad that the school director has tentatively accepted the post.

Sparhof, May 13, 1932

Dear Mama, Hilde, and Reinhold,

Now Whitsun has come already, and I want to wish all three of you a very happy and beautiful Whitsun celebration, with some nice quiet and festive days. If only the weather would also turn a bit nicer! It is still quite cold and rains a lot. They are almost despairing on the farm because they are not able to make any headway with the tilling.

I still wanted to write you about the first of May. It was a wonderful day. We got up very early with the children – all of them, big and small – and formed a procession.

The girls all wore flower garlands in their hair and the boys carried flower bouquets bound to long sticks. We marched through all the houses and sang a May song at the door of every room in which someone was still sleeping. Then a child went in with a spring posy. It was a lot of fun and everyone enjoyed it very much. We started singing at six o'clock and were finished at seven. We had also learned several new May songs. Then a colorful maypole was put up in the yard. Unfortunately we couldn't have a children's festival because of the flu.

The preparations for Whitsun and the experience of Whitsun are wonderful. In our evening meetings we are reading the teachings on Pentecost about the Holy Spirit that were written by the Hutterite Brothers. Some of them are very old manuscripts from the sixteenth and seventeenth centuries. The preparations actually began on Ascension Day. I believe that several guests will be coming for Whitsun. In general there are many more people coming to us now, and there are often very good discussions at our mealtimes.

There are also several new people here now, mainly volunteers who came to help us with the work in the farm and garden. Two of them – a gardener and a kindergarten teacher who had worked in a kindergarten in Berlin run by a Protestant mission organization – have decided to commit their lives to the community here. Now there are almost one hundred of us and probably soon that number will be complete. Of Emi-Margret's parents, only her mother will be here for Whitsun; at the moment they are both in Bad Liebenstein for about three weeks. Emi-Margret's father has to undergo an eye therapy there. Due to an accident he has completely lost his vision in one eye.

The nightwatch's rules are being strictly observed again. All lights must be out by ten o'clock. Work starts quite early in the mornings, especially for the men. I get up sometime between five o'clock and five-thirty–sometimes earlier, depending on my plans for the day. The children only get up at 6:45, so one can get a lot done in these morning hours. We have real plumbing up here, but the water is in quite short supply and hardly sufficient for the large demand. It is particularly difficult in summer. Sometimes–of course just when one needs it most urgently–one can stand at the faucet for a long time before a drop comes out. We don't have electric lights up here. We use kerosene lamps or candles. I seem to have a special gift for breaking the glass cylinders of the lamps.

I'm so glad that Mr. B. made such a good impression on you. It would be very encouraging if he turned out to be really competent. You found a very good solution with Miss Z. I hope you will find other good replacements as well. If only Hilde would recover more quickly. What did the doctor say? How expensive is such a radium-activated compression? I hope you will have a few quiet and relaxing Whitsun days so that you can at least get a bit of rest. But the news from the attorney is certainly not encouraging. I just don't quite understand why we were assigned the costs. When are the summer holidays scheduled this year? Will it be July and August again? How is the order and discipline in the house now? Hopefully there aren't such great difficulties anymore.

My children give me much joy, although there are naturally also difficulties every now and again. We are hoping to take in four more orphans (siblings). The social worker responsible for them would like to come now at Whitsun to inspect the Sparhof. We are hoping very much that something will come out of it.

But I should stop now. I hope my letter will arrive in time. Warm greetings and kisses–I think of you with much love.

Your Anni

Have a wonderful Whitsun celebration.

DIARY

Ascension Day, May 1932

> We could never fully comprehend you,
> your image paled
> before our daily activities.
>
> You were only a name to us, a rumor,
> intellectually we thought of you
> as the great and universal one.
>
> And so you were obscure to us
> like a meaningless painting.

Sometimes, in rare moments
we had a deep inner sense
and we believed we were bound to Him.
We sensed that someone was calling us
to life in God alone.
Yet you were not real to us, not deed and judgment.
You didn't come like a streaming light
into the darkness of our night.

We remained imprisoned in human pettiness.
Our eye did not recognize the starlight
that would lead us on.

Brazen and impudent,
we believed we could do without you,
forgetting that we were created by your hand.

And yet you alone were the eternal!

And then, of a sudden, through your nearness
our eyes were opened wide
and your brilliant light overwhelmed us.

We were captured by the glow of love,
yours, yours for ever, spirit, soul, and everything,
burning in love for you.

Everything that is bound and fettered in us
longs for redemption, to be raised up in you.

Uniting love will proclaim
that you are in us, and we are in you.

On the Küppel, May 1932

Wide, boundless world before me!
The creator holds it in his hands.
For it is you who quickens everything,
brings life into death.
Infinite creative will, grant
that nothing petty remains in us,
that we are purified of anything that leads astray
and rest in you, God, alone.

Sparhof, May 27, 1932

My dear Mama, Hilde, and Reinhold,

At Whitsun we had wonderful summer weather, and
as a result many people hiking in the area dropped in to
visit us. There were also some who stayed on a bit longer.
We had very lively and interesting discussions with
these guests in the evenings, which we all enjoyed very
much. The following week was a very busy work week,
especially for the farm and garden. We had nice warm
weather, which made it a very good time for this work.

The countryside looks beautiful now. The meadows
are just covered with flowers. The cherry trees bloomed
right at Whitsun. The apple trees are still in full bloom.

Everything looks so lovely. The garden is now yielding lots of rhubarb and radishes.

This time I'm also sending you some of the globe-flowers that turn the meadows here yellow. I hope they will arrive fresh and in good condition. The wreath of mountain-everlasting flowers is for Hilde's room. The whole Küppel is full of them. Every time you see them in your room they should remind you that I think of you all with very much love and don't want anything that separates to come between us, even if our paths are different. You can be sure that I certainly don't want to cut all ties with you from my side, and that nothing is farther from my heart than allowing an estrangement to come between us. However, there does have to be clarity about our different ways and there can be no blurring of the two. And so I really plead with you to recognize my way as a way, even if you can't personally accept and approve of it. I believe that it's the only way. But over and above that it must be possible to have understanding and love not only amongst us as closest relatives but also in the broadest sense as from person to person. If we here only wanted to live in proud self-assertion we would never dare to go out to other people to share our message with them.

We really cannot compare our relationship to one another with the break that happened between Mama's siblings. And I truly hope that something like that will never happen between us. But certainly I can hold on to this alone–that my life be lived only in the complete clarity and purity of this eternally old yet eternally new way.

I was also very happy to receive Mama's greeting for Sunday.

Lilo Lühr visited us here last week from Wednesday to Monday. I spent a lot of time with her. She will probably come again in the fall. It just happened to be very beautiful weather.

I have to stop now because I have to start giving the children their baths. I hope you will receive this greeting by Sunday.

Greeting you all very warmly,

your Anni

I was so glad to hear that you were able to visit the relatives in Weimar. The Fröbel writings, the little picture book, and the sweet little pictures made me especially happy. Unfortunately, the little vase was broken. The six of us were very interested in all the goodies.

I greet all three of you very much with a kiss,

your Anni

9.

Consequence

The year 1932 was difficult not only for Anni and her family. The German economy was in shambles, with industry at a standstill and over six million unemployed. The Weimar Republic was disintegrating, and although Hitler had been defeated in a bitterly disputed election with President Hindenburg in May, his angry rhetoric was whipping up emotion at ever larger rallies.

For the members of the Sparhof community, apprehension about the political future of Germany was tempered by confidence in the cause to which they were committed. There was also an abundance of work at the growing community; most of Anni's attention was taken by her work with the children. The foster children, many of whom came from broken families, could be difficult to care for, and education was discussed repeatedly at members' meetings during the spring of 1932. Eberhard Arnold wrote an article summarizing these discussions. "The aim of our education," he wrote, "must be to awaken and strengthen in every child all that is good, pure, and

genuinely childlike, together with a joy in the beauties
of nature and unclouded comradeship, so that the atmo-
sphere of community gains a foothold in each individual
child." The theme of children and education had taken
on a special significance for Eberhard that spring: his and
Emmy's first grandchild, Heidi, was born to Emi-Margret
Zumpe and her husband Hans on May 14.

Anni responded to this article in a letter to Eberhard
Arnold, who was spending several weeks at Bad Lieben-
stein, a town near Keilhau, receiving treatment for his
injured eye.

Sparhof, June 4, 1932

Dear Eberhard,

How surprised I was to receive your letter. I know
how extremely busy you are. Your letter brought me such
great happiness. Thank you very much.

Last night we read your essay on the education and
care of children. Once again I felt so thankful that I can
live with the children and take part in the work with
them. It seems like a great miracle to me. Of course I also
realized again how easily I can let myself be guided by
my own human will. One often cuts oneself off from the
true connection to the soul of a child and to what is most
pure in them by using human force in an attempt to get
the appearance of a result. We constantly need to open
ourselves completely to the great, living, active power
of the Spirit. Only in this way can we too come deeply
into contact with the godly and good Spirit within the

child – the Spirit that brings all things into being. Only when we let ourselves be filled completely by this life-giving Spirit can we guide a child with love, confidence, and mutual understanding. Ultimately, of course, when this happens it is in spite of us.

The responsibility we have toward the children is sometimes overwhelmingly great, and can only be carried in faith. This faith is most strongly needed when we encounter unchildlike and impure things in a child that want to lead him or her away from a childlike oneness with the good and godly toward what is evil. Sometimes it almost seems (and this can make us feel quite help-less) that even within a little child the battle which every person wages between the light of good and the darkness of sin has already ended in an irrevocable victory for the powers of evil. The question is always whether we ourselves then yearn so fervently to be filled to the same degree by the other power that we become able to detect and find the godly inner light even in the spirit that may seem to be the most unchildlike and farthest from the good. We may then connect with and encourage this little spark. Only since little Heidi Maria was born have I really understood what childlike wholeness of being and oneness with the source of all good is, and what it means to acquaint a child with life and things in this world. A little soul like hers is something so pure, inno-cent, and inviolate that one can only stand continually in awe before the miracle of life made new. It will be so wonderful when you are back here again and can see her. Emi-Margret is also looking forward to it so much.

You wrote about wanting to visit my mother if possible. I would be very happy about that and very grateful to you. It would reassure me very much. But of course I don't want you to give up so much of your time – which is always in such short supply – for a personal matter. The row with my family is by no means over yet. On the contrary, it seems as though my relatives are farther away than ever from reaching acceptance and a solution. They increasingly view the matter only from the perspective of our personal relationship to one another and therefore are increasingly unable to comprehend my conduct. Yet the only reasons I can give for this step are, of course, not subjective ones. There simply are no other explanations. They increasingly refuse to recognize the facts I have set before them, saying that these are questions of one's world view, ideals, or principles that don't carry much water when it comes to one's actions and the direct relationship of person to person. And they say that the love naturally shown to one's nearest kin can only be called love if it is backed by deeds – especially if one of those concerned is in need. And that this proof of mutual love must come before anything else. And because they themselves are now in need, this is the only way they are able to view it all.

The truth is that, after years of very demanding work both physically and emotionally, my mother now needs more rest and relaxation as she grows older. It is also true that my sister is very ill. She has been ill for many years and is able to rise above her sickness only with great effort. But now her condition seems to be worsening steadily, so much so that my brother genuinely fears for her life.

I am well aware that my refusal to help in the way my brother wishes would be a heavy blow for my sister, and my mother too. The consequence could quite likely be the very thing my brother fears. But on the other hand I obviously can't give up this new life. As you of course know, it isn't a selfish life for my own sake, but my relatives naturally believe I'm only looking for and finding my own personal spiritual gratification in it. Because we have had such a close family relationship, I'm sure you will understand how much I truly wish to be able to find a positive solution for them as well. And the question arises as to whether it may and can be that by turning to a life under God and to the active love which grows out of such a life, one at the same time may cut off and destroy the love – and therefore the inner existence – of those to whom one has previously believed oneself strongly bound and who now find themselves – this is the dilemma – in dire straits. The issue at hand is not merely a matter of a personal separation, which one would be able to bear through faith, but rather it is a matter of the hardship – and then even the increased hardship – of the other person. And I cannot believe that it is right for one love to injure the other. It also can't be that a life lived for people – for all people – can be right if through it some are wounded to their very core. And therefore I also think that a positive solution has to be found. It just hasn't yet become clear to me how to go about this – I mean, the actual, practical way to this solution. I have written you so much about this firstly because you asked me to, but also because I have grappled with this question for a while already and it has lately become especially acute for me.

But of course I don't want to let this personal matter occupy me too much, because it becomes clear to me again and again how little and unimportant all personal matters are and must be in light of the great cause – that which has already come to pass and that which is happening right now. And yet, on the other hand, it is essential that these personal things are resolved and rectified so that one's entire strength can really be used in service to the great task, without reservations. And the great and beautiful thing is precisely that the certainty of the reality of God's spirit and the life of Jesus Christ alone can lift us above all personal matters to where the freedom of a life lived under God and in discipleship to Jesus Christ can begin. It is becoming clearer and clearer to me how strong, active, and real the power of God's spirit is. That has actually always been the question – the search for the absolute and therefore uncompromising reality of God that can leave no path open other than that of discipleship. To me it was never a question of the various consequences that such a discipleship entails, questions of possessionlessness, conscientious objection to war, voluntary poverty, or social justice. These things certainly belong to it, but almost as purely logical, intellectual implications. For me it was about finding nearness to God and believing in this nearness; believing that a person can be so encompassed by it that they can move from an intellectual understanding and awareness to a complete surrender of all strengths and powers. My doubts about faith in God stemmed from a belief in relativism which was the only thing left after I failed to find any other answer in my search for the meaning of life.

And so it is a tremendously great thing that all of us here are allowed to experience the movement of the Spirit ever anew. We experience it firstly through the worship meetings in which by turning to God – something that each must do individually – strength for unity in purpose and deed is given. It's like a small sending out of missionaries within the circle of the community, where from the common source of strength each one is sent out into the fight in day-to-day matters, in the substance of the daily work.

Secondly, however, the movement of the Spirit is exceptionally noticeable now in the encounters with guests and volunteers who have been so numerous since Whitsun. Something really happens at these discussions that can't be created by mere words or rhetorical skill – so much so that, especially on that one Whitsun day, one of the guests, a student from the Habertshof who had originally given only a perfectly dry and factual review of work in a work camp, could suddenly abandon all of that in an attempt to reconcile his most personal and intimate convictions with those of this life. And this evening too, in a meeting with the new printers, it was once again evident that even though there is not yet a full affirmation of this way, the beginning of an understanding and leaning toward the power that brought about this communal life is certainly arising.

And we ourselves must also realize again and again that this seemingly so basic certainty comes from such tremendously great power and grace. As such, we can never become indifferent and hardened toward it, taking it all for granted in complacent, self-satisfied, and narrow acceptance. If we would, life in community would no doubt become merely mechanical, a dogmatic legalism.

And I think – if I have understood it correctly – that all of this will be overcome, and we can find a childlikeness of heart in which we continue to experience the miracle and grace of the gift of unity ever anew and with the greatest longing. Then our dedication will also be perfect, without any legalism. Then the experience of Whitsun would certainly become a new reality every day.

I just received a copy of your article about the work with the children. I was very happy, and I am especially thankful to you for it because this essay has become so important to me in finding the right approach.

Warm greetings,

Anni

Hilde was spending some weeks convalescing in a spa town near Keilhau.

Sparhof, June 25, 1932

My dear Hilde,

How happy I was when I received your dear little note from Gernrode. I was especially glad to hear that you find it so nice and pleasant there.

The summer landscape here with its dark green beeches and firs and meadows rich with flowers is really something exceptional – but so completely different from our Thuringian woods and countryside. Right now we are having such horrible cold weather, but a week ago it was so wonderfully warm. The hay-making began during that time and they still managed to get the hay in nice and dry.

We've already picked lots of big, red wild strawberries with the children, and now the ones in the garden are also starting to ripen. Are there also wild strawberries in Gernrode? I really hope so much, my dearest Hildelina, that your stay there can make a big difference in your recovery and help you become stronger. But you just have to be a good girl and make a real effort to relax and be lazy.

Last Tuesday was a very special day for us. We celebrated the summer solstice and at the same time the twelfth anniversary of the community. We all gathered in the dining room at 5:30 p.m. At our communal meal there was lots of singing and people spoke or read aloud. We were gathered until shortly before nine. We then met at 9:30 and went up to the burial ground together where a fire was lighted. We formed a circle of about eighty people

around the fire. It was so big that you couldn't recognize
the faces of the people standing across the circle. It was an
extraordinary feeling to know that so many people were
bound together in such a deep communal experience. At
the end Emi-Margret's father spoke about the meaning
of fire in our inner life. Hand in hand in a long line, we
then went down the hill to our community. It was a long
chain: the last ones were still up on the hill when the first
were already standing in the yard and singing.

Today Emi-Margret and I received very shaking news,
namely, that Maria Keller, the director of the school in
Thale, died in a bad car accident on June 23. It was really
staggering news. As you know, the entire school stands
and falls with her. To be sure the notice said that the
school will carry on in her spirit, but I can hardly imagine
that. These days must have been extremely upsetting and
trying for everyone there in Thale. Emi-Margret and I
want to write to Fräulein Wichon, who was actually the
closest to her.

The whole community has taken longer walks of three
or more hours together these last two Sundays. Everyone
who could went along, including the bigger children.
We would then find a nice place in a meadow or pasture
to sit and sing or talk to one another. Emi-Margret's
father often spoke on some subject or read aloud to us.
Last Sunday he read from the history of the fledgling
Anabaptist movement in Reformation times. We were
in an especially beautiful place, all the mountains of the
high Rhön lay before us in the distance. Such communal
walks are always very nice – one can converse with all

sorts of different people and become better acquainted with them.

Yesterday evening Reinhold phoned me from Keilhau, primarily because the bank needs me to sign something. He asked me to come, not only for that but also to be able to completely clarify all other matters. I raised the question in the members' meeting, and after discussion we decided that the best time for such a trip would be in about a week, around the 4th or 5th of July. I wrote this to Reinhold, who wanted to call again tomorrow. So I am planning to arrive around those dates to visit you for a few days. I am so endlessly happy that I will be able to see you all once again. I hope so very much that we will come close to one another again, also by discussing and clarifying everything, which is definitely necessary. Inwardly we do of course belong together even though our callings are different, so we ought to be able to find a great love and understanding toward one another over and above everything. I naturally think of you all the time, and also speak often with Emi-Margret and others about you and Keilhau. Only one thing must remain: the new way must remain pure and clear.

But now good-bye, enjoy Gernrode to the fullest. The glowing yellow arnica flower brings you my deepest love and a kiss

from your Anni

We will see each other again soon!!!

Later the same day, Anni wrote to her mother.

Sparhof, June 25, 1932

My dear good Mama!

The strawberries are starting to ripen now, and so begins the great canning season. We have fairly large strawberry patches, one of them a whole field. Until now we have been processing rhubarb, stewing and juicing it, and making it into jam. Most of the jam is used immediately since we would otherwise have to buy it. It doesn't even need that much sugar – I think about one third of the weight. We already have a lot of lettuce and spinach, mainly from the cold frames, and plenty of red and white radishes. It is of course quite difficult at the moment to feed the ever-increasing household. When I came we were not quite eighty people and now we are 110. And now we almost always have twenty-four to thirty guests with us. It is also becoming more and more difficult to find accommodation for them all. For the summer, a kind of youth hostel arrangement has been set up for them in the attic of one of the new houses. Most of these new people help with work on the farm or in the garden as well as in the print shop. The women guests help primarily in the kitchen. There the most curious combinations of people meet, some of whom come from the Youth Movement, but certainly not all. They often have very interesting discussions there.

In warm weather the babies lie outside in little laundry baskets that are lined inside with blue material and have a collapsible canopy of the same blue linen. It always looks so cheerful under the green trees. This Monday three new children are coming to our children's community – two brothers, aged four and eight, and a twelve year old girl – for an initial trial period of three months. The two boys are called Daniel and Johannes. I will probably be their main caregiver. A young seventeen-year-old girl is also coming; she would like to work at least part-time with the children. At the moment I have only the four oldest boys living with me. Due to his special difficulties, the youngest one was placed alone with another family.

We now have one more person working with the children again, namely the nice arts and crafts teacher with whom I had already worked when I first arrived. It is very nice to have her because it means we can spend a little more time with the children. These last few days were so nice and warm that I took the girls up to the Küppel at 6:00 o'clock in the morning for gymnastics. That was a lot of fun. Now it's so cold, wet, and foggy that we can't do it anymore.

You should once see how our meadows around here look now. They are so colorful and completely filled with flowers! Arnica is blooming in some of them. I haven't seen any columbine or wild salvia yet, but there are a lot of little harebells.

I wrote all the details of my planned visit to Reinhold and also Hilde. But I can't yet give you an exact date. It will be so wonderful when I'm with you all once again and we can speak about everything. It's not too much longer until then.

Looking forward so very much to seeing you, and greeting you with a warm kiss,

Your Anni

Thank you very much for your loving letters and greetings.

Anni was lovingly welcomed home to Keilhau by her family. But the discussions of the future of the Keilhau school and family financial arrangements that were the reason for her visit did not go well. It was inconceivable to her family that their daughter could leave a decades' old tradition and calling. Anni described the trip in her diary.

D I A R Y

July 5 to July 8 and 9, 1932

The trip home in order to bring about a full discussion and clarification, especially in regard to property.

Strength and clarity and unflinching firmness are so necessary. The unflinching clarity and integrity of the way must be upheld so that one can speak of this way in all humility and modesty.

To be filled with inner joy through strength.

And again strength – strength – strength that penetrates everything.

July 5, the first day of the trip

When Hans Zumpe left us in Eichenried, I realized that now I could only go on, there was no turning back.

To go on is also completely my will, only it is so difficult, so infinitely difficult.

The entire trip was under the sign of the inner preparation of what was to come and therefore of concentrating on what I should witness to and what was given to me by the Spirit of the church. But the tensions kept increasing, becoming almost unbearable.

Human strength means so very little. It breaks down completely and can do nothing, nothing at all. If we depended on it, we would have to drown in helplessness and uncertainty. We ourselves do not know the way out, we are so weak.

So on that evening shortly before Rudolstadt I was almost beyond my strength. The impossibility of mastering the task was so enormous that I was in utter despair. And yet I was aware all the time that it had to be, that I could not weaken. All the time my urgent and fervent request is, "Give me your strength, give me your Spirit! My longing for that is so endlessly great. Without it I'm completely at a loss. Without your help I don't know where to turn. Help me! Help me all the way to your victory!

What else am I to do?
Strength, your strength, fill me!

On Wednesday, July 6, there was a talk with Uncle Hugo. He said: Jesus wants a discipleship in the conditions we are in, as they are given to us; we should do the duties in the station in life into which we are born, especially our duties to our own family. For our parents are representatives of God. And–he said–it is sin against God and against Christ if I want in the first place to do what there is to do somewhere further off, in the Sparhof community. It is said, "Love your neighbor," but who could be closer to us than our own immediate family?

There was a fierce argument. (He wanted to leave right away.)

God–God help me!
Help me to say everything I have to say!
I am in great need.

The tension was so strong, so unbearable. To have to be with these very beloved people and not be able to speak out until the right moment. To have to make myself cold and hard so as not to be a hypocrite and so as to remain completely clear and firm. And yet I know that the inner separation is there and that it has to be. We no longer have any connection in our life, our doing, thinking, acting–in anything in us that is directed toward the future. Nothing is left but the faith that this will one day be healed.

But in all that separates, there is one thing that remains– the deep, primal love of mother for child and child for mother, two beings that once were completely one; the child had rested beneath the mother's heart and was carried by her in love and born with pain and joy. To know this and yet have to carry out this step causes untold tension and pain.

On Friday, July 8, at 10:30 in the morning, I told Mama, Reinhold, and Hilde that I had decided to resign from the family partnership altogether so that I can belong completely to the other.

As to what followed then, I can hardly grasp the fact that I was able to look on with a calm and unaltered expression. Mama in her deep agitation broke out with the shattering cry: "Then you aren't my child anymore, then you aren't my child anymore." And then she went completely to pieces. Then there was the walk with Reinhold, during which we talked with great outward calmness but deepest inner agitation. "How will you answer for the fact that one day you will have to stand at your sister's grave as her murderer? How can you take the responsibility for this step upon yourself at all?"

"I take this responsibility on myself in faith in the new life that has been shown to me," I answered. And there was no bridge to span the gap between us.

Then at home I told Mama and Hilde once again that I would be true to this way and would leave in the afternoon. And then—such a shattering breakdown—Mama fell weeping on her bed, and Hilde threw herself on top of her. I stood there very calm, unable to say a single word; only my hands were trembling, and icy shivers ran down my back. When I went back to her later, she was standing there quite broken, weeping, completely shattered. And I realized how mother-love overcame everything: she tried to blame it on everybody else except me; she refused to believe that her child wanted to break away from her. Hilde took me by the arm and shrieked in my face, "How can you look on and see your mother standing there so completely shattered? Don't you have any heart in your body, can't you see–this is your mother. Do you want to make our suffering still worse? Mama weeps day and night and finds no rest. How can you look on? I can't bear it anymore, how restless her nights are. I can't bear the suffering anymore." And she shook me by the arm as if she were trying to wake me up.

I said goodbye then and crept secretly out of the house like a thief, left the village, and ran all the way to Rudolstadt as if I were being chased. And in the hours that followed, these images pursued me and wouldn't leave me. My strength to bear it was just about gone.

"He who honors father or mother more than me is not worthy of me, and he who honors brother or sister more than me is not worthy of me."

Then I came home to the Sparhof, and the spirit of the cause and of unity was there again, and that gave me new strength.

But inwardly I am still pressed and weighed down by it all and can't overcome it so easily. But I don't want to burden anyone with it. I know that others, like Emmy, Else, Eberhard, Dora and Nils, and the Bollers, had it a thousand times harder. But I can't force myself to get over it. Then too, there is the frightening, tormenting feeling that I was not strong enough or firm enough. I wasn't able to express myself in the right way or with the right power. I was inadequate in how I represented the cause, also in words. I was not even able to adequately clarify and put in order property and financial affairs. And that is the thing I find hardest and most depressing–that I served the cause so poorly. This trip did not bring things a single step forward; I spoke and acted only in a weak and unclear way. It would probably have been much better if I hadn't gone.

I still can't get back into the rhythm of community life at all.

10.

Radicalism of Surrender;
Radicalism of Deed

Anni had only been back at the Sparhof for a few days when she wrote again to her family.

Sparhof, July 11, 1932

Dear Mama, Hilde, and Reinhold,

In a very wonderful way we are experiencing every day anew how God is leading and blessing this way and this work. In the past few days five or six new people have felt so deeply gripped and moved by this way of life and by the strength that can come down to mankind, that they could do nothing else than say yes to it with their whole hearts. They have now turned their whole lives towards this newfound way. And also the way in which we are led and provided for in all outward matters lets us feel extremely powerfully how surely we are guided and governed by a divine power. And everything given us outwardly in the physical necessities of daily life, as well as inwardly through renewal of people, constantly strengthens our confidence in the belief that, firstly, this is the way we must follow and that, secondly, no one who has heard the call and wants to continue to obey it can turn back. Rather, they must pour themselves and their entire life into this new life.

And I only wish so much that you might one day be able to experience the great, sustaining strength and power given to us through the experience of complete inner unity. Then you would be able to understand that the only desire of this strength, which originates in unity, is to continuously build new unity. This strength demands nothing other than that we surrender ourselves for unity. It was only possible for me to overcome the pain of parting from you because I believe in and have been touched by this strength. And I strongly believe that one day – even if not yet now – we will be able to agree deeply and come to unity in this matter. This alone, then, is the only possible help I can give you and long so much to be able to give you: the help that gives us strength to bear every burden, and also every other matter, in faith in the power of unity.

And in this faith and with this plea I greet you all most warmly.

Your Anni

Anni had become a novice shortly after her arrival at the Sparhof. The novitiate was a time of testing and deepening understanding of the community and its basis. Now she was to be accepted into the circle of full members, the "brotherhood." Membership in the brotherhood was offered only to those who had shown the seriousness of their dedication to their calling. Aware of this, Hilde wrote a lengthy letter to Irmgard Blau, begging her to use her influence to convince Anni to leave the Sparhof. Irmgard declined. As she later recounted, "I didn't know what to say about it. What was I supposed to do? I couldn't advise for or against it – of course, I didn't know who they were either." Later, in a letter to Eberhard and Emmy Arnold, Anni's mother beseeched them to release her daughter from her commitments. Eberhard Arnold, in his response, attempted to explain to Frau Wächter the nature of Anni's commitment and calling.

July 20, 1932

Very dear Frau Professor Wächter,

Even before receiving your card just now, I had promised my dear wife, Emmy, who always thinks of you with special love, that I would write to you. Your letter to my dear wife was unfortunately written under such erroneous assumptions that it could only have been answered by speaking face to face. Through Annemarie, we have repeatedly requested you to visit us, and both my wife and I would gladly be prepared to visit you in Keilhau, if by doing so we might be of service to you and your dear Annemarie.

If only we might explain to you from heart to heart how the decision of your and our dear Annemarie came about! But this is a religious mystery that can be explained only by God's personal word, spoken by him to the heart of a human being. No one among us has talked Annemarie into the decision to join this life. We would reject completely any decision to join that was brought about by human persuasion. One can only enter our life community when one is directly called and chosen by God himself. For this reason, I believe that you, your dear daughter Hilde, and your son Reinhold will only be able to understand Annemarie when you listen to the religious source and motives really deeply and inwardly. Annemarie has tried in a number of letters, and at length, to reveal her decision to you in her own language and way, as she alone can do.

When you write, dear Frau Professor Wächter, that there is no mutual commitment, that is true insofar as we here know no human attachment. So your request that I release Annemarie and make it possible for her to return home has come to the wrong address. Annemarie, and also I, stand to the church, and this church is for us the cause of God and of the Holy Spirit, a call to live in complete community, a call that is more than ever necessary today. As you can see confirmed in Annemarie's letter, Annemarie made a commitment as a novice on January 31. She gave her word to God in the presence of the gathered church to belong completely and forever to the discipleship of Jesus here at the community, and that she belongs to full community of life and of work, and gives all her gifts, possessions, and capacities to the work of faith. She made this declaration voluntarily and on a deep foundation. We would be doing Annemarie's inner life a great wrong if we doubt this declaration even for a moment. So I beg you to understand that we can only ask God together that he might show us, through his good, pure spirit in complete unanimity, what must take place.

You write that your and our Annemarie "is now so dejected, whereas she used to be happier." This is due, as you yourself have noticed, only to her love for you, for she suffers indescribably because you do not understand her step in faith – indeed want with all the means at your disposal to reverse it.

If you, dear Frau Professor Wächter, could for one moment accept in your heart that this is a matter of the deepest religious happiness of your beloved daughter, and that opposition in the family can only deepen a real religious decision, in that hearts may be deeply grieved and distressed and still not be able to give up their faith; if you consider that out of religious motives fatherland and home, father and mother, and even life itself were very often given up and forsaken; and if you understand in your heart that a religious experience of this nature has taken place in Annemarie you will reconcile yourself to it in motherly love and not refuse your child your blessing. And Annemarie will ask you for this blessing again and again because it means so much to her. We other community members, who have been gripped by the same call of God and placed on this way, also want to do all we can to bring about mutual understanding.

So we ask you if we may do you and your daughter Hilde the small service of sending you our sister Dora Sääf to nurse her. Certainly your dear daughter will not find the dress of our sister as disturbing as when Annemarie wears it. It will not be possible for either of them to lay this dress aside, for the religious significance of the church and community is expressed by unity in dress. Thus we ask you to be so kind and tell us when our sister Dora may come. I am also prepared to visit you personally, if my visit may help to bring peace. It would not be good for Annemarie's feelings or those of her sick sister Hilde were she, as a member of the community with her unchangeable decision of faithfulness to the community and community dress, to care for your daughter. This will certainly be more possible at a later date, when the agitation in the family over her unexpected decision has calmed down somewhat.

I wish from my heart that you might often be with us to hear with what love and respect we think of Friedrich Fröbel's life work and of the fruitful work of your father and grandfather, and how we agree with the deepest direction of the founding of Fröbel's work. The difference is only that we here see in the full community of the first Christians, and in the divine justice and peace of the kingdom of God, the only real flowering of all the thoughts that have influenced Pestalozzi, Fröbel, Barop, and others. Because my great-grandfather Ramsauer was also one of the first co-workers of Pestalozzi, doubtless I might find with you and your dear son Reinhold a much better objective understanding than seems to be the case now.

We ask you once more to visit us and Annemarie here, or if I may go to you.

Yours most respectfully,

Eberhard Arnold

DIARY

July 31, 1932

Last week, on July 27, Mama and Hilde came here to fetch me home. Hilde had actually gotten up from her sickbed so that Mama wouldn't have to travel alone. It was simply heartrending to see them standing before me again, begging and pleading. Never has my mother's life lain open before me as in those hours. Starting at an early age, she served at Keilhau, toiling with utmost self-denial under difficulties and hardships. She bore her children with great pain, and for the sake of the cause had them cared for largely by others. Then Otto, on whom great hopes had been set, fell in the war; then Papa died, and a few years later Grandmother too. The burden of the task remained, but she had to carry it alone more and more.

She continued to give all her energies with a view to the time when her children would relieve her of the task and she would be able to rest after all her care and toil. And now this! This hit her harder, she said, than when Otto fell. I could hardly bear seeing Mama and Hilde—a picture of deepest inner need and despair and extreme helplessness. "You rob us of all joy in life, you make our life joyless and sorrowful!"

And in the face of this I had to remain almost silent. Not in the sense of agreement, nor a rejection, nor a backing down; no, not for one second, even though my heart was torn and bleeding. But I felt completely powerless to do anything or help in any way, incapable of speaking one single word of inner help or comfort; on the contrary, I must have appeared downright hardhearted and loveless.

D I A R Y

August 2, 1932

What does it mean to be accepted into the brotherhood? I used to think it meant the same as baptism and happened at the same time.

Through this step the fact of total surrender to the cause, of immersing myself completely, is reaffirmed. And it means, more strongly than in the novitiate, accepting the consequences of this act and taking complete responsibility for the cause. Not only being dedicated, but also being determined to be answerable for what springs from this attitude in every contact with others within and outside of the community. It also means wanting to help carry all weaknesses and failures, whether of a personal or objective nature. A desire to be included in the complete unanimity that is given through the spirit is needed. And it means bringing this unanimity to expression in the relationship to others, as completely as humanly possible, by witnessing to it in life and deed.

This step means renewing my vow of inviolable, joyful

faithfulness to God and his spirit. If to begin with it was a matter of letting go, of dedication and a growing faith, now it means certainty, my whole bearing, and responsible deeds that become visible in accordance with our confession. Our actions and representation of that which we have promised is so often clouded and distorted through human weakness and inability. For this reason we can actually only be accepted into the brotherhood in faith and trust in the guiding Spirit who gives himself to us when we are willing to come before God in poverty and humility.

Sparhof, August 4, 1932 (postcard)

Dear Reinhold,

I heard from Mama how well you did in your doctoral exam. I am so happy about that and hope it may be a good omen for your future work. I was so surprised how quickly the day of the exam arrived in the end.

Hopefully Mama and Hilde got home safely and without incident, and hopefully Hilde's condition wasn't worsened by the journey. I was certainly very happy that they visited me, even though I could not and cannot do what they request. And that is what continues to distress me so much: that we are completely talking past each other. And that is why it is so near to my heart that you would once be able to completely understand – and wish to understand – the deepest reasons why I had to act in this way and in this way alone.

The days here are currently very lively and eventful. The most completely different types of people arrive here every day, seeking an encounter with the cause.

But for now goodbye and very warm greetings to you all from

your Anni

I have been helping quite a bit with the canning lately – we are hardly able to tackle it all.

D I A R Y

August 6, 1932

God alone is the truth, without beginning or end! Only through him do we live. We belong to him, to him alone. We are allowed to belong to him, to serve him with all the strength of our heart, spirit, and body. We stand before him as children. Without him we are nothing, without him there is only darkness and despair. Oh, may the night never overcome us again, the darkness of being separated from you! Help us to the light, to the light of your love, that we may be set on fire by your light, to be burned and consumed like a candle. The "I" is burned up and only you, you alone fill us. May our hearts always burn in love to you! May we always live in the shattering of your presence! May we never grow cold! Take from us the death of a cold heart, the coldness of the intellect! May our hearts be torn in pain if they do not belong to you. Give us glowing, burning souls that no longer seek ourselves but recognize and desire you alone! Give it to us, I beg and plead with you! Everything is extinguished and we are colder and harder than the hardest stone if you are far away. I can do nothing more if you don't help. Everything is shattered, I cannot go on. May your power come, your power! Give it to us, give it to us completely so that our hearts are cut by the sharp knife of your love and your will. Bring the torment to an end! Come to us with your Spirit. Give us your power. I am poor, I am nothing. Only you exist, you, God!

In the past I sometimes wished for an unconscious radicalism in which my heart would be filled to the outermost cells with one thing alone, that I would no longer be aware of myself, that all torment and seeking, all doubt and skepticism would come to an end.

Now it has come over me, something I never believed I would find. To be sure, it is not an unconscious radicalism in the sense of ecstasy or intoxication; it is a radicalism of surrender, a radicalism of deed.

DIARY

August 7, 1932
Accepted into the brotherhood.

With her life's course now fixed, Anni was determined not to let the rift with her family become wider. In the following months, the exchange of letters continued with greater intensity than before. In addition to continuing to explain the nature of her vocation, Anni used her letters to describe the day-to-day life of the Sparhof in the hope that her family would come to understand how her faith affected all aspects of life.

Sparhof, August 12, 1932

My dear, good Mama and Hilde,

I received your dear package two or three days ago. Many, many thanks for it. You thought it all out so lovingly. The little bunch of carnations was still completely fresh when it arrived. The new dress has such a pretty pattern and also fits me well. And the ankle socks are also nice. My children joined me in strengthening themselves with your delicious cookies and enjoyed them very much. Thank you both for all the love I felt again through this.

Now it is finally warm and sunny here. Yesterday the last of the hay was brought in and the rye harvest began. There's also a lot to harvest from the garden now – beans, peas, carrots, cucumbers. We are canning a lot every day now, also lots of vegetables. The vegetables are being preserved mostly in cans made of material similar to the marmalade pails. These cans can be reused every year. They only have be sealed with a new lid by a special machine each year. We are also making lots of jam. It's all turning out very nicely. I often help with the canning now, that's why I know so much about it. While picking wild raspberries we can often observe deer. They are quite numerous up here, but we seldom see any hares or rabbits.

At the moment we have many guests again. This time there are also more young women, several students who came here through Emi-Margret's brother. They attended university in Tübingen with him. They seem to be very nice. A new teacher has been here since the beginning of August. She's helping in the school, especially in the elementary classes. She has a very lively and refreshing manner and the children like her a lot. She was very involved in the singing clubs of the Youth Movement and is extremely musical. She actually wanted to study music. We hope that she will help us liven up our singing again, and indeed, we have already had several very enjoyable singing evenings with her.

There are around 120 people here now, including guests, and that number increases continuously. Sometime soon Dr. Isemann, the director of the home for the mentally ill in Nordhausen, will visit us along with several of his co-workers. He wants to find out more about the work here, especially the work with the children. He is one of the most eminent educators in the field of educational therapy. One of our more difficult children was there until just recently. And several other children may possibly be sent there for observation and therapy. He has a great understanding for our work and was very considerate towards us.

And now to close with, thank you all again so much for everything. I'm sending you a little kiss and greet you all.

Your Anni

The whole Küppel is now covered with heather and golden thistles.

On August 21, 1932 the Keilhau Blätter carried the following notice:

On July 25 of this year instructor Reinhold Wächter of Keilhau, son of the late Prof. Dr. Wächter, who passed away in 1922, passed his Ph.D. exam at the University of Jena *magna cum laude* on the basis of his thesis "Anastasius Grün's political poetry. An analysis of his style and thought."

Sparhof, August 23, 1932

Dear good Mama and Hilde,

I was very happy to receive Hilde's last letter and thank her very much for it. Everything you wrote interested me very much.

The last eight to fourteen days have been extremely hot, so the harvest proceeded in leaps and bounds. We hardly knew what to harvest first – hay or barley – and in the garden lots of beans, and raspberries in the woods. A large part of the household was kept busy all day long snapping beans to be blanched and pickled in cans. In the evenings after dinner we often sat all together and sang with great spirit while we snapped. We've harvested about three and a half hundredweight of raspberries from the woods, and there was a group of us out in the woods again this morning. We've made lots of juice and jam with them.

It was often so hot during the day that we had to stop working in the midday hour. But the worst thing was the water shortage–water is anyways very scarce but during the drought we often had water only in the morning or very late at night. If the heat had lasted any longer we probably would have run out completely within a few days. But luckily it got much cooler again yesterday.

On Sunday evening after dinner we went out to the Küppel under one of the big beech trees. There was a large bank of black clouds in front of us that was constantly lit up by sheet lightning. It looked just beautiful. We lit two torches and Emi-Margret's father read a very important chapter from the revised edition of his book *Inner Land.* It was a wonderful evening. We lay around the two torches, above us the great old beech tree whose branches were so numerous one couldn't see the sky through them at all anymore, and in front of us the bank of clouds in which the sheet lightning constantly played.

At three o'clock in the morning the storm hit us with great force. Lightning and thunder came from every direction, and it was often so bright that one could see the edge of the forest far in the distance. But it didn't strike us. The children weren't scared at all; they lay in their beds very quietly and peacefully.

We've recently been going out often in the evenings and also on Sunday mornings to read or have discussions outdoors. It's always very beautiful and everyone enjoys it. We have often had very lively discussions lately–it always depends on the guests. At the moment we have a communist with radical Marxist leanings staying with us for a while; this makes for excellent and very lively discussions. We also had a student of economic science with us who represented capitalism, and of course they clashed. Then we also had a Mennonite who couldn't understand the communist at all, and yesterday two people came from a settlement representing vegetarianism and the back-to-nature movement. Such discussions often continue late into the night even though they actually aren't supposed to because work starts so early each morning. The dining room is too small for that many people and it's also always difficult to find enough space for them to stay the night, but we are certainly happy that so many people come to us.

I've been part of the brotherhood circle for about fourteen days now.

Those of us who work in the children's home have been getting together during the coffee breaks for quite a while already. It's two teachers, another young girl and I. We always have a very nice, relaxing time while we drink our coffee.

Hopefully your good weather there has lasted, so that Hilde can spend lots of time lying outdoors on her nice deck chair. When it was so hot here our children went several times to a pool in Hutten, about an hour away. They were always very enthusiastic about going there.

But now goodbye. I greet all of you most lovingly with a little kiss from your

Anni

In late August, Anni received word from home that Hilde's health had declined further. She shared this news with the members of the community during a meeting, asking for prayers and advice. Eberhard Arnold, saying that he considered Hilde's situation to be of "utmost inner concern" to the community, asked Anni to write to her family to again offer that a sister from the community, Alice Löffler, travel to Keilhau to provide help with nursing. This offer was not accepted, and Anni's uncle, a pastor, was sent to reason with her.

DIARY

September 4, 1932

On August 31, Uncle Hugo Wächter came to visit me. He said he had heard from Frau Pastor Kuntze that Hilde had only a few weeks to live. And he hoped to impress me deeply by this news.

I can hardly grasp it, it pursues and torments me day and night. How will it be, how will it happen, if this really comes about? I don't want to think about it, but it oppresses and torments and tortures me every time the activities of daily work let up for a moment. The responsibility is so great and our strength is so small. My conscience is not yet fully justified through my faith. Faith is such a precious thing, and its complete authority is constantly being interrupted by our doubt, our fear, our need. The truth of this bitter way grows plainer all the time. And the hardships of the way often become so gigantic, they grow as dense and impenetrable as a wall, so that we feel we are missing the right path and will lose our way. And when our emotional strength is used up, discouragement tries to set in. It is the same with the children's work. I get so downhearted about everything that I am at my wit's end.

But we must not, we must not lose courage. That would be sin. We must venture forward nevertheless. For otherwise everything will be lost. And I see more and more clearly how terribly, how inhumanly hard it was for Jesus in Gethsemane to drink the cup to the dregs.

In the next weeks, Hilde's health improved slightly, although she remained an invalid. Frau Wächter and Reinhold continued to implore Anni to return home.

Sparhof, September 11, 1932

Dear Mama, Hilde, and Reinhold,

I've been meaning to answer your letters as soon as possible but unfortunately it wasn't possible until just now. But now this morning's phone call gives me further reason to write you.

I don't know if I was able to make it clear and obvious to you through my letters that it really is possible for people to experience fundamental inner changes that can truly transform their lives completely. I don't know if you were able to recognize that I had encountered this kind of powerful inner decision. And I'm also not sure whether my letters conveyed to you that this type of religious experience is more than the rescue of an individual soul for its inner peace; that its repercussions go out beyond the confines of an individual's spiritual impulses and feelings. It wants to encompass and penetrate the whole of life–everything within mankind and everything that mankind can accomplish–without compromise or exception in either the mental and spiritual or the physical and material sphere.

If you are able to understand that, it will also be clear to you that I cannot serve the cause here wholeheartedly while at the same time and with the same dedication throwing myself into the tasks and goals you see before you there in Keilhau. It simply is not possible to really serve in two completely different callings.

And yet there's one thing I'd like to repeat to you again most emphatically: with this step I dissociate myself only from our three-way family business partnership with its collective tasks and assignments. I cannot and do not ever want to separate myself from the three of you on a personal level. And you shouldn't think that I look down on your way of life because I cannot share in it. I'm sure you'll agree that one person can feel deeply connected to another regardless of whether or not they both walk the same path in life. How much more possible that should be if these people happen to be next of kin, as is the case with us! If it were not so, every individual or group of like-minded people might as well retreat into the cloister of their own way of life and sequester themselves there. But we of course want to come closer to one another. Naturally, I cannot stray from the direction of the path clearly defined by my life-goal for the sake of this recognition. And just as you would not want to give up what you have recognized as right and important in your life-vocation, so too you would not want me to do anything that would be contrary to my life-goal.

But apart from that we certainly do want to remain just as closely bound to each other, parent to child and sibling to sibling, as we have been until now. For it would be only a very weak love if it would wish to cease where paths diverge. It ought to be strong enough to respect different paths, binding people to each other over and above them, in order to perhaps bring them together completely in the end.

And so in this sense I greet all three of you very deeply and with intense love, wishing so much that we might eventually come to this very last thought.

Your Anni

Sparhof, October 28, 1932

My dear, good Mama and Hilde, dear Reinhold,

You made me so very happy with the birthday parcel, so lovingly packed and thought out! Everything looked so beautiful that I hardly dared open it. Many, many thanks! It also arrived exactly on my birthday. The little flowers are still standing on my dresser. The birthday cake looked so delicious. We devoured it the next afternoon with the children and teachers at a very happy birthday snack. The day of my birthday was also very nice. The children sang me a birthday song and Emi-Margret had made everything so beautiful and festive for me in her room. I was so happy for the wonderful things and will put them to good use. Now I'm well equipped for winter. The children are also delighted with the little duck, especially since they've discovered that it can turn its head. Warm thanks to Reinhold, too, for his loving birthday greeting.

We have very nasty winter weather here now – it rains without stopping and of course there's mud everywhere because of it. The sun only seldom shows a glimpse of itself, and then only for minutes.

We are already diligently starting to work on Christmas projects with the children now. It's a lot of fun for everyone.

Now I want to tell you about the wedding of the Swedish couple. On Saturday afternoon we drove them to the registrar in a festively decorated coach. While they were gone we worked in feverish haste to clean, cook, decorate, and arrange everything beautifully. The dining room was decorated with very colorful leaves and the last of the flowers. They returned at seven o'clock and then we had a festive meal. We sang many songs – folk songs and also more serious ones. Several things were read aloud. The children had practiced several very sweet performances, even something in Swedish. It was a very beautiful, joyful evening.

The real wedding celebration was the next morning at ten o'clock, first with the brotherhood, then publicly with the whole household. Some very important passages about the meaning and symbolism of marriage were read from the manuscripts of the Hutterian Brothers. Following that was a celebratory meal. After the meal the couple left. They are spending their honeymoon in their homeland, Sweden, and will be gone for about three weeks. Those remaining sat together over coffee until about 6:30, when everything was over.

It was so nice that I could spend time with Reinhold last Thursday. I was very happy about his visit, and the time together went by very quickly.

But now goodbye. I thank you many, many times for all your love and greet you most lovingly with a kiss.

Your Anni

Sparhof, November 24, 1932

My dear Mama, Hilde, and Reinhold,

Very many heartfelt greetings to all three of you for the first of Advent. The little wreath and the little Christmas pictures are meant to bring you a bit of Christmas spirit and light. And I wish you a very beautiful and joyful Advent.

When we awoke yesterday everything was white with snow. Unfortunately this enchantment didn't last too long, instead it soon turned itself into quite a muddy mess.

Did you celebrate All Souls' Day last Sunday with the students? And were there such beautiful wreaths on the graves again this year? We had a little festive meeting around Else von Hollander's grave up in the burial ground. The burial ground is situated at almost the highest point of our property. It's only now being properly laid out. A wall of about half a meter high will be built around it, using the large stones found in meadows and fields around here. A belt of fir and birch trees will be planted around the outside of the wall, and seven linden trees inside it. A little clearing will be made in front of the burial ground. And around that is the spruce forest. Part of the work is already being done by volunteer work camps.

Last Sunday another little girl was born, a little Esther. She is the first sister for three brothers, who are very pleased about her. That means there will soon be eight little baskets in the baby room, six girls and two boys. It looks very cheerful.

The print shop is also in the midst of intensive work right now. They're printing postcards for Christmas with texts taken from the second century, and then they'll print flyers about the various books of our publishing house, mainly the ones that highlight the *Quellen* series. These flyers still have to be finished before Christmas so that our books can still be advertised everywhere before Christmas.

Will you also make the first of Advent a little bit festive and Christmassy? I really hope so. Next time I will tell you how everything was here.

But for now goodbye, sending you a very warm little Advent and Christmas greeting,

your Anni

Sparhof, December 2, 1932

My dearest Mama, Hilde, and Reinhold,

Your Christmas package arrived last Saturday. When I opened it late that evening the fragrance of Christmas wafted around me. It looked so beautiful and mysterious inside, just like Christmas. You packed it so beautifully. The pine branches are hanging over my bed and I put up the little angel that same evening. I enjoyed the Christmas goodies with the children. Thank you so much for your loving cards.

I want to tell you how we celebrated the first of Advent. During the night from Saturday to Sunday we suddenly heard singing. Five angels came in and sang to us, carrying burning candles in their hands. It was so sweet to watch the children wake up and gaze in wonder at the angels. The five angels sang to all the families and went into all the rooms where people were sleeping. They brought Advent wreaths to everyone. All the children were so sweet.

I had secretly hung a little wreath and a Christmas picture above the bed of each of my children. In the morning they were hardly to be contained. We had breakfast all together in the dining room, and the children ate in the children's house. A huge Advent wreath hung in the dining room and one just like it in the hall of the children's house. The dining room looked beautiful, everything decorated with pine branches. There was a large transparency, and at each place at the long tables was a twig of pine with a red candle. During breakfast each person lighted someone else's candle and said a few words or suggested a Christmas song. Eventually all the candles in the whole dining room were lit. In this way, our breakfast lasted until well into the morning. At noon the children sang some Christmas carols they had learned. All day there was a very Christmassy atmosphere everywhere. In the evening we practiced our nativity play. It was a very nice first of Advent.

The following week there was feverish activity all over, especially in the print shop and the woodworking shop, where the crèches and bookmarks are made. In the print shop flyers had to be finished for our individual books so that the books would get to the Christmas market. For various reasons the work had been held up, and Christmas is drawing closer, so now everyone has to work extra hard. Many people helped who usually don't have anything to do with this kind of work. The flyers all had to be folded and creased, several thousand of each. At the same time we had to practice the nativity play, which many people were involved in. We want to perform it on the second Sunday of Advent for the community. It is hard to coordinate these different things and to get all the different people to be there.

I am very eager to hear how you celebrated the first of Advent and how the singing in the musicians' guild went. I hope you are having a very nice Advent and Christmas. Unfortunately the weather doesn't feel like Christmas yet; everything is muddy. But there was frost again last night.

I must close now and get to work. All the best to you all, and a big kiss from your

Anni

Sparhof, December 20, 1932

My dear Mama, Hilde, and Reinhold,

First of all I wish all three of you a very happy, joyful, and meaningful Christmas celebration. I am with you in my thoughts and keep imagining what you are doing and how you will celebrate together. I hope very much that the Christmas days are wonderful and peaceful for you. Have you found your Christmas tree yet?

By the way, I heard a rumor that the Keilhau Christkind came and left a gigantic package. I can't wait to see it. Every day packages and parcels arrive from all sides for various members of the household. Everybody is in a Christmas mood, especially the children of course. The next few days will pass in no time.

To our great disappointment, the snow has all melted and everything is muddy again. Hopefully it will snow again.

Did you manage all your Christmas preparations – shopping, wrapping, baking cookies and Stollen, cleaning? Tell me everything, I want to hear all the details. I hope Hilde's wicked pain lets up during Christmas. Is the principal there, or any other teachers?

Goodbye for now. I still have to wrap my package so

it arrives in time. So now here is a heartfelt Christmas greetings and a loving kiss from your

Anni, who is thinking of you very much

D I A R Y

December 31, 1932 to January 1, 1933

When I arrived here at the beginning of January 1932, everything stood under the strong and living impression of Else von Hollander's death. What was proclaimed through this death and in this death gave a direction not only for me personally but for the whole work of the community. It accompanied us throughout the whole year. It gave courage for the great decisions and tasks as well as for everything that affected us personally. It accompanied us on our mission.

It was as though the gate to eternity had been opened and we had been granted a glimpse into the wonderful glory of the other world. However little of it we were able to sense, yet it was so strong that it overwhelmed us small human beings completely. Our hearts are hardly strong enough for it. Else is our strong, living connection to the upper church. Her words describing what she was already seeing with different eyes moved and shook us to the depths. It is eternity. It is a path that comes to us from the throne of eternity and leads back into the glory of eternity. Eternity in God gives shape to every moment of the present, even if we are not part of it. Woe to us if we lose these moments. This is the only way. If we are not willing, we will remain outside. But it is a path that brings the light beams of the other world directly to us, with no separation of space or anything in between, immediately sharp and clear from eternity to eternity. We are permeated and inflamed, and we want to surrender and devote ourselves completely so that we don't miss God's moments.

God almighty, through your spirit in Jesus Christ, give us the glow of love, the power of unity of your love, that we burn like blazing fires in expectation of your kingdom. Give us a strong faith – let our faith not weaken. God all-powerful, let our hearts be shattered every moment, that the power of your mission and message might tear hearts open, that we might endure shame and disgrace, suffering and death with you, Jesus Christ, that nothing at all is too difficult for us in order to honor the truth. God, give us the power, come to us through your spirit, we plead and implore you!

In the face of all torment and pain in the world, we have the certainty of the one way. That is the only reason that our responsibility in face of the need of the world doesn't bring us to despair but can and must give faith for the future. We believe in you, God, and in your son Jesus Christ, who comes to us through your Holy Spirit. We believe you and we want you and the glory of your kingdom. Sometimes our prayer is a lie, because we do not have a burning longing, a hunger for your love, your justice, your kingdom.

We don't want to come to you out of mere habit. We want to be like people dying of hunger and thirst, driven by our need for your Spirit to uninterrupted, concentrated wakefulness, so that our raised hands, the hands of our hearts, are ready to be filled, to receive and accept your Spirit.

Weariness and sleepiness come again and again like a darkening cloud and there is so much that hinders us.

When will clarity, certainty, and power come? When will the light come? God, I pray you, grant it, give it to us!

God's Spirit, God's power
come, come!
There is nothing beside you!

Afterword

A recurring theme in Annemarie's writings is her search for a "fixed point" – an absolute worth staking everything on. As the letters printed in the last section of this book show, this search found fulfillment in a life of unreserved commitment to Jesus. With this commitment, her other longings – for true relationships, for education that focused on what was of God in a child – also found fulfillment. But in a way, this was only the beginning of the story.

Following Hitler's election as Chancellor in May 1933, the Third Reich gained in power from week to week. To the members of the community, it seemed as if madness had descended on Germany. Eberhard Arnold, as leader, expressed their united opposition to the Nazi ideology in correspondence to various officials, including Hitler himself. Nor was this opposition ignored. On November 16, 1933 at around eight o'clock in the morning, the Sparhof – which by then consisted of around 120 adults and children – was surrounded by over 150 armed SS, local police, and Gestapo who searched the property. Annemarie was in the children's house when the raid occurred and later remembered:

I was in my room in the children's house when I noticed soldiers going into every house. They ordered everybody to stay in their rooms. I had to stay in there the whole time they were on the community searching all the rooms, behind furniture and under mattresses, pulling out letters and whatever they could find. They were actually looking for weapons but of course they did not find any. They took away a lot of literature, especially books with red covers, because red stood for communism and they thought we were probably communistic. But many of the books were just art books.

Soon it became impossible for community life to continue in Germany. When it seemed certain that a Nazi teacher would be assigned to the community school (as had already happened at the school in Keilhau), the members decided that the children should flee the country rather than be subjected to Nazi influence. Annemarie and another teacher accompanied the children first to Switzerland and then to a new community location in the Liechtenstein Alps. There they were soon joined by the children's parents as well as the young men of military age who, as conscientious objectors, were in danger of imprisonment or execution for refusing to serve in the armed forces.

Emi-Margret's younger brother, Heinrich, who was then attending an agricultural college in Zurich, was a frequent visitor to the Alpine community when his studies allowed. He and Annemarie had come to know each other well in the community youth group and during semester breaks when he helped as a teacher in the school, and they were engaged on Christmas Eve of 1934. The letters they exchanged during the fifteen months of their engagement would fill another volume. Only days after their wedding on March 24, 1936, the young couple found themselves refugees again, this time bound for England, where they and other members of the community made their home for several years until escalation of the war prompted migration to Paraguay.

In their forty-four years of marriage they had nine children, including two daughters who died in infancy. Their life together, and that of the community, is described in Homage to a Broken Man, *a biography of Heinrich Arnold by Peter Mommsen.*

Annemarie never met Irmgard Blau again after becoming a member of the community. Irmgard became involved in a Nazi youth organization during the 1930s and was appointed to a position of leadership. But her girlhood dedication to seeking truth stood her in good stead. She wrote to Emi-Margret after Annemarie's death in 1980:

Right from the beginning I had a strong inclination against Nazism, but I could not give any reasons for this feeling. I also had no political experience, which unfortunately was the case with most of my contemporaries. Then I had a decisive experience in 1937 in a home for mothers where I was working. There I had to choose publicly, and repudiated Nazism. Only afterward did I realize that it wasn't me who chose but that God chose over me in that he gave me courage and strength to confess to him.

Irmgard married the following year, and through her husband became involved in the Confessing Church, which was active in opposition to Hitler. Her letter to Emi-Margret continues:

I never forgot Annemarie and I was always sorry that I lost contact with her and the fate of the community. I had no more news after they emigrated to Paraguay. How glad I would have been to see Annemarie again. The two years I spent in Naumburg were also very decisive for me.

When I visited Annemarie at the college in Thale, I already sensed that you were taking my place. Because of that I did not like you too much. Of course now in old age one looks at many things differently, and today I feel a heartfelt joy about Annemarie's way of life and that such a community exists.

Annemarie's family gradually came to accept and respect her chosen calling. Reinhold, writing from communist East Germany to Annemarie after the death of her infant daughter Marianne in 1948, wrote, "We were especially moved that all those who live with you were able to share your joy—and then also your sorrow; it fills us with a deep respect. *Here people inform against one another, go behind each other's backs, and take advantage of each other, so that sometimes one is in despair over the great inner need our people are in. So what you write of such love of each for the others seems like something out of another—and a better—world. And the fact that good is still so active should give us strength to hold on."* Annemarie rejoiced in the restored relationship with her brother, who with his wife later escaped East Germany for Berlin, where he dedicated his life to teaching and to editing and publishing the works of Friedrich Fröbel. They remained close until the end of her life. Two months before her death she wrote to him, *"In my effort to describe my new recognitions clearly, I was sometimes too stiff, cold, and loveless. Later I was very sorry for this. Nonetheless I am very thankful how close we have come since then."*

This reconciliation was not immediate. For the Wächter family, life in the years after Annemarie left home was difficult. Annemarie visited Keilhau again in October 1933 to celebrate her birthday with her mother and sister, whose condition had deteriorated badly. The night before her birthday Annemarie spent in conversation with Hilde, who asked her how it was possible for Else von Hollander to die in such peace. Annemarie told her what she knew of Else's last days, assuring Hilde of "the strength and assurance that come from faith, which can overcome all fear of death and bodily pain." Early the next morning Hilde died quietly and peacefully at the age of thirty-four.

Now Reinhold was the only child remaining at home, and he with his mother attempted to carry on in the Fröbel tradition at the Keilhau school. But in May 1933, a Nazi principal was appointed to the school, and in 1939 it was closed, along with all other private schools in Germany. Reinhold was dispossessed and later drafted; he served in a transport unit and was later held as a prisoner of war in Austria.

Hedwig Wächter, who had formerly managed a household of over one hundred and fifty people, now lived alone in a series of tiny apartments, horrified and frightened by the political developments in Germany. "There is an atmosphere of excitement and agitation as the prospect of war becomes more and more a probability," she wrote to Annemarie in September 1938. "Whether we will see each other again this year is in God's hand; irrational and unreasonable times, hard times lie ahead of us." She and Reinhold visited Heinrich and Annemarie at the community in England when their first child, Emmy-Maria Hedwig, was born in August 1938. Oma Hedwig delighted in this first grandchild—"such a joy to me, the little dear with her soft little cheeks"—and both she and Reinhold came to understand more of the community during their visit. But Emmy-Maria was tiny and weak, and she died of an infection when she was only three months old.

When a second daughter, Roswith, was born in 1939, the approaching war made it impossible for Frau Wächter to travel to England. She never saw Annemarie again. After

*the community was forced to leave England for Para-
guay in 1941, letters were the only connection between
mother and daughter. Frau Wächter rejoiced in the
news of each new grandchild, celebrating their far-away
birthdays and childhood achievements. Her own letters
were filled with the devastation and turmoil that had
engulfed Europe. As the war escalated, even the fragile
link of correspondence was threatened. The letters that
were delivered took over six months to arrive, but most
letters were lost—twice during the war, Frau Wächter had
to wait for two years to receive a letter from Annemarie.
But despite the distance, their love and understanding for
each other only grew stronger. Frau Wächter wrote to her
in 1946 as "my most beloved Anni-child (you will always
be that for ever and ever)."*

*Then in April 1947 Annemarie received a letter from
Reinhold. Hedwig Wächter, weakened by wartime starvation, had died alone at her kitchen table, "while she
had been preparing our supper, caring like a mother up to
her last moment as she had done her whole life."*

*The close-knit family, the long-established school at
Keilhau, the Youth Movement idealism—all the things
that had shaped Annemarie's early life were gone, broken
by the war. But to her, holding to the "fixed point" she had
found, they were replaced by a far greater gain. Annemarie's is a living legacy. In place of her family, thousands*

of people today seek to remain faithful to the same call that drew her. In place of the Keilhau school, the Fröbel-inspired education she and Emi-Margret introduced to the community lives on in dozens of schools and kinder-gartens worldwide. And in place of Youth Movement idealism, there is a life where (as she wrote) "the anticipation and promise of the kingdom of God translates into living deeds, and where unity results from this one Spirit."